OVE · MARRIAGE · LOSS · JOURNEYS

FRIENDSHIP

FRIENDSHIP

EDITED BY

Shena Mackay

J. M. Dent London

To my friend
Valerie Foster

First published in Great Britain in 1997
by J. M. Dent

A CIP catalogue record for this book is available
from the British Library.

ISBN 0 460 87930 8

Typeset at The Spartan Press Ltd,
Lymington, Hants
Set in 10/11½ Photina
Printed in Great Britain by
Clays Ltd, St Ives plc

J. M. Dent

Weidenfeld & Nicolson
The Orion Publishing Group Ltd
Orion House
5 Upper Saint Martin's Lane
London, WC2H 9EA

CONTENTS

INTRODUCTION

Friendship seems to be a universal human need, and one which is shared by some other animals, who display altruism and companionship towards their own kind, and extend it to us. The prisoner finds solace in taming a bird, a solitary child will make friends of caterpillars and confide in a toy, the lonely child invents imaginary playmates, the very survival of street children depends on their friends; and who, if faced with the choice of betraying country or friend, would not hesitate, for a moment at least, before coming to a decision? Male friendship has been celebrated through the ages in legend and literature, in the gruff manly symbiosis of, say, Conan Doyle's Holmes and Watson and John Buchan's heroes, and in the buddy movies of the present day. The biblical Naomi and Ruth are still quoted as a potent example of women's friendship, and, nearer our own times, yet almost as remote in their mores, the innocently passionate chums of 1930s boarding-school fiction could express their affection for one another unselfconsciously, balancing insouciantly on the rim of the well of loneliness without a thought of falling in.

The field of friendship is vast, and the boundary line between its territory and that of love is vague. The poems chosen here from the First World War say as much about soldiers' comradeship as they do about the animals they portray; and Angus Wilson, the grandmaster of social embarrassment, writes painfully of friendship thwarted by class distinction in the Second World War. Brigid Brophy's post-war young people experience love, betrayal and heart-break in Venice; Aamer Hussein's dream-like story evokes a Java of the heart. In Nann Morgenstern's sharply contemporary 'The Befriender', which explores several layers of friendship, women are brought closer by the impending death of one of their group, and find their own courage through hers.

Perhaps because first friendships can be the most intense that we experience, the literature of childhood offers an embarrassment of riches; in this selection, Richard Wilbur brings the dynamics of a psychological power-struggle to a ballgame, while Elspeth Sandys shows a small act of playground heroism that begins a lifelong relationship, and Muriel Spark's malicious twins destroy one. As Bulwer-Lytton observed, 'There is no man so friendless but what he can find a friend sincere enough to tell him disagreeable truths', and Liz Lochhead's account of a chance meeting with an old school 'friend', corroborating his theory, will provoke a wry laugh of recognition from many readers. A similarity in age is not necessarily a criterion of friendship, as two of the pieces illustrate: Walter de la Mare's haunting, and haunted, Miss Duveen is an eccentric old lady who befriends a little boy and in Elizabeth McCracken's remarkable first novel a librarian is astonished by her love for a very tall boy indeed. Each one of the writers represented in this book – those mentioned above and their illustrious fellows – gives his or her unique version of a subject that engages us all at some time in our lives.

But how do we choose our friends, and why? Or did they pick us? Who has not wondered at some time, 'Why is this person my friend?' Fleur Adcock addresses the questions that perhaps we don't care, or dare, to ask, in her amusing and yet serious poem that makes a fitting epilogue for this small tribute to the enduring power of friendship.

WILLIAM SHAKESPEARE

'Blow, Blow, Thou Winter Wind'

Blow, blow, thou winter wind,
Thou art not so unkind
　　As man's ingratitude;
Thy tooth is not so keen
Because thou art not seen,
　　Although thy breath be rude.
Heigh-ho! sing, heigh-ho! unto the green holly:
Most friendship is feigning, most loving mere folly.
　　Then heigh-ho! the holly!
　　　This life is most jolly.

Freeze, freeze thou bitter sky,
That dost not bite so nigh
　　As benefits forgot:
Though thou the waters warp,
Thy sting is not so sharp
　　As friend remember'd not.
Heigh-ho! sing heigh-ho! unto the green holly:
Most friendship is feigning, most loving mere folly.
　　Then heigh-ho! the holly!
　　　This life is most jolly.

MURIEL SPARK

The Twins

When Jennie was at school with me, she was one of those well-behaved and intelligent girls who were, and maybe still are, popular with everyone in Scottish schools. The popularity of boys and girls in English schools, so far as I gather, goes by other, less easily definable qualities, and also by their prowess at games. However, it was not so with us, and although Jennie was not much use at hockey, she was good and quiet and clever, and we all liked her. She was rather nice-looking too, plump, dark-haired, clear, neat.

She married a Londoner, Simon Reeves. I heard from her occasionally. She was living in Essex, and once or twice, when she came to London, we met. But it was some years before I could pay my long-promised visit to them, and by the time I got round to it, her twins, Marjie and Jeff, were five years old.

They were noticeably beautiful children; dark, like Jennie, with a charming way of holding their heads. Jennie was, as she always had been, a sensible girl. She made nothing of their beauty, on which everyone felt compelled to remark. 'As long as they behave themselves—' said Jennie; and I thought what a pretty girl she was herself, and how little notice she took of her looks, and how much care she took with other people. I noticed that Jennie assumed that everyone else was inwardly as quiet, as peacefully inclined, as little prone to be perturbed, as herself. I found this very restful and was grateful to Jennie for it. Her husband resembled her in this; but otherwise, Simon was more positive. He was brisk, full of activity, as indeed was Jennie; the difference between them was that Jennie never appeared to be bustling, even at her busiest hours, while Simon always seemed to live in the act of doing something. They were a fine match. I supposed he had gained from Jennie, during their six years of marriage, a little of her sweet and self-denying nature for he was really considerate. Simon would stop mowing the lawn at once, if he caught sight of the old man next door asleep in a deck-chair, although his need to do something about the lawn was apparently intense. For Jennie's part, she had learned from Simon how to speak to men without embarrassment. This was something she had been unable to do at the age of eighteen. Jennie got from Simon an insight into the mentalities of a fair variety of people, because his friends were curiously mixed, socially and intellectually. And in a way, Simon bore within himself an integrated combination of all those people he brought to the house; he represented them, almost, and kept his balance at the same time. So that Jennie derived from Simon a knowledge of the world, without actually weathering the world. A happy couple. And then, of course, there were the twins.

I arrived on a Saturday afternoon, to spend a week. The lovely twins were put to bed at six, and I did not see them much on the Sunday, as a neighbouring couple took them off for a day's picnicking with their own children. I spent most of Monday chatting with Jennie about old times and new times, while little Marjie and Jeff played in the garden. They were lively, full of noise and everything that goes with healthy children. And they were advanced for their years; both could read and write, taught by Jennie. She was sending them to school in September. They pronounced their words very clearly, and I was amused to notice some of Jennie's Scottish phraseology coming out in their English intonation.

Well, they went off to bed at six sharp that day: Simon

3

came home shortly afterwards, and we dined in a pleasant hum-drum peace.

It wasn't until the Tuesday morning that I really got on close speaking terms with the twins. Jennie took the car to the village to fetch some groceries, and for an hour I played with them in the garden. Again, I was struck by their loveliness and intelligence, especially of the little girl. She was the sort of child who noticed everything. The boy was quicker with words, however; his vocabulary was exceptionally large.

Jennie returned, and after tea, I went indoors to write letters. I heard Jennie telling the children, 'Go and play yourselves down the other end of the garden and don't make too much noise, mind.' She went to do something in the kitchen. After a while, there was a ring at the back door. The children scampered in from the garden, while Jennie answered the ring.

'Baker,' said the man.

'Oh, yes,' said Jennie: 'wait, I'll get my purse.'

I went on writing my letter, only half-hearing the sound of Jennie's small-change as she, presumably, paid the baker's man.

In a moment, Marjie was by my side.

'Hallo,' I said.

Margie did not answer.

'Hallo, Marjie,' I said. 'Have you come to keep me company?'

'Listen,' said little Marjie in a whisper, looking over her shoulder. 'Listen.'

'Yes,' I said.

She looked over her shoulder again, as if afraid her mother might come in.

'Will you give me half a crown?' whispered Marjie, holding out her hand.

'Well,' I said, 'what do you want it for?'

'I want it,' said Marjie, looking furtively behind her again.

4

'Would your Mummy want you to have it?' I said.

'Give me half a crown,' said Marjie.

'I'd rather not,' I said. 'But I'll tell you what, I'll buy you a—'

But Marjie had fled, out of the door, into the kitchen. 'She'd rather not,' I heard her say to someone.

Presently, Jennie came in, looking upset.

'Oh,' she said, 'I hope you didn't feel hurt. I only wanted to pay the baker, and I hadn't enough change. He hadn't any either; so just on the spur of the moment I sent Marjie for a loan of half a crown till tonight. But I shouldn't have done that. I *never* borrow anything as a rule.'

'Well, of course!' I said. 'Of course I'll lend you half a crown. I've got plenty of change. I didn't understand and I got the message all wrong; I thought she wanted it for herself and that you wouldn't like that.'

Jennie looked doubtful. I funked explaining the whole of Marjie's act. It isn't easy to give evidence against a child of five.

'Oh, they never ask for money,' said Jennie. 'I would never allow them to ask anyone for anything. They never do *that*.'

'I'm sure they don't,' I said, floundering a bit.

Jennie was much too kind to point out that this was what I had just been suggesting. She was altogether too nice to let the incident make any difference during my stay. That night, Simon came home just after six. He had bought two elaborate spinning-tops for the twins. These tops had to be wound up, and they sang a tinny little tune while they spun.

'You'll ruin those children,' said Jennie.

Simon enjoyed himself that evening, playing with the tops.

'You'll break them before the children even see them,' said Jennie.

Simon put them away. But when one of his friends, a pilot from a nearby aerodrome, looked in later in the evening, Simon brought out the tops again; and the two men played

5

delightedly with them, occasionally peering into the works and discussing what made the tops go; while Jennie and I made scornful comments.

Little Marjie and Jeff were highly pleased with the tops next morning, but by the afternoon they had tired of them and gone on to something more in the romping line. After dinner Simon produced a couple of small gadgets. They were the things that go inside musical cigarette boxes, he explained, and he thought they would fit into the spinning-tops, so that the children could have a change of tune.

'When they get fed up with "Pop Goes the Weasel",' he said, 'they can have "In and Out the Windows".'

He got out one of the tops to take it apart and fit in the new tune. But when he had put the pieces together again, the top wouldn't sing at all. Jennie tried to help, but we couldn't get 'In and Out the Windows'. So Simon patiently unpieced the top, put the gadgets aside, and said they would do for something else.

'That's Jeff's top,' said Jennie, in her precise way, looking at the pieces on the carpet. 'Jeff's is the red one, Marjie has the blue.'

Once more, Simon started piecing the toy together, with the old tune inside it, while Jennie and I went to make some tea.

'I'll bet it won't work now,' said Jennie with a giggle.

When we returned, Simon was reading and the top was gone.

'Did you fix it?' said Jennie.

'Yes,' he said absently. 'I've put it away.'

It rained the next morning and the twins were indoors.

'Why not play with your tops?' Jennie said.

'Your Daddy took one of them to pieces last night,' Jennie informed them, 'and put all the pieces back again.'

Jennie had the stoic in her nature and did not believe in shielding her children from possible disappointment.

'He was hoping,' she added, 'to fit new tunes inside it. But it wouldn't work with the new tune . . . But he's going to try again.'

They took this quite hopefully, and I didn't see much of them for some hours although, when the rain stopped and I went outside, I saw the small boy spinning his bright-red top on the hard concrete of the garage floor. About noon little Jeff came running into the kitchen where Jennie was baking. He was howling hard, his small face distorted with grief. He held in both arms the spare parts of his top.

'My top!' he sobbed. 'My top!'

'Goodness,' said Jennie, 'what did you do to it? Don't cry, poor wee pet.'

'I found it,' he said. 'I found my top all in pieces under that box behind Daddy's car. My top,' he wept. 'Daddy's broken my top.'

Margie came in and looked on unmoved, hugging her blue top.

'But you were playing with the top this morning!' I said. 'Isn't yours the red one? You were spinning it.'

'I was playing with the blue one,' he wept. 'And then I found my own top all broken. Daddy broke it.'

Jennie sat them up to their dinner, and Jeff presently stopped crying.

Jennie was cheerful about it, although she said to me afterwards, 'I think Simon might have told me he couldn't put it together again. But isn't it just like a man? They're that proud of themselves, men.'

As I have said, it isn't easy to give evidence against a child of five. And especially to its mother.

Jennie tactfully put the pieces of the top back in the box behind the garage. They were still there, rusty and un-touched, in a pile of other rusty things, seven years later, for I saw them. Jennie got skipping ropes for the twins that day and when they had gone to bed, she removed Marjie's top from the toy-cupboard. 'It'll only make wee Jeff cry to see it,' she said to me. 'We'll just forget about the tops.'

'And I don't want Simon to find out that I found *him* out,' she giggled.

I don't think tops were ever mentioned again in the household. If they were, I am sure Jennie would change the subject. An affectionate couple; it was impossible not to feel kindly towards them; not so towards the children.

I was abroad for some years after that, and heard sometimes from Jennie at first; later, we seldom wrote, and then not at all. I had been back in London for about a year when I met Jennie in Baker Street. She was excited about her children, now aged twelve, who had both won scholarships and were going off to boarding schools in the autumn.

'Come and see them while they've got their holidays,' she said. 'We often talk about you, Simon and I.' It was good to hear Jennie's kind voice again.

I went to stay for a few days in August. I felt sure the twins must have grown out of their peculiarities, and I was right. Jennie brought them to meet me at the station. They had grown rather quiet; both still extremely good-looking. These children possessed an unusual composure for their years. They were well-mannered as Jennie had been at their age, but without Jennie's shyness.

Simon was pruning something in the garden when we got to the house.

'Why, you haven't changed a bit,' he said. 'A bit thinner maybe. Nice to see you so flourishing.'

Jennie went to make tea. In these surroundings she seemed to have endured no change; and she had made no change in her ways in the seven years since my last visit.

The twins started chatting about their school life, and Simon asked me questions I could not answer about the size of the population of the places I had lived in abroad. When Jennie returned, Simon leapt off to wash.

'I'm sorry Simon said that,' said Jennie to me when he had gone. 'I don't think he should have said it, but you know how tactless men are.'

'Said what?' I asked.

'About you looking thin and ill,' said Jennie.

'Oh, I didn't take it *that* way!' I said.

'Didn't you?' said Jennie with an understanding smile. 'That was sweet of you.'

'Thin and haggard indeed!' said Jennie as she poured out the tea, and the twins discreetly passed the sandwiches.

That night I sat up late talking to the couple. Jennie retained the former habit of making a tea-session at nine o'clock and I accompanied her to the kitchen. While she was talking, she placed a few biscuits neatly into a small green box.

'There's the kettle boiling,' said Jennie, going out with the box in her hand. 'You know where the teapot is, I won't be a minute.'

She returned in a few seconds, and we carried off our tray.

It was past one before we parted for the night. Jennie had taken care to make me comfortable. She had put fresh flowers on the dressing-table, and there, beside by bed, was the little box of biscuits she had thoughtfully provided. I munched one while I looked out of the window at the calm country sky, ruminating upon Jennie's perennial merits. I have always regarded the lack of neurosis in people with awe. I am too much with brightly intelligent, highly erratic friends. In this Jennie, I decided, reposed a mystery which I and my like could not fathom.

Jennie had driven off next day to fetch the twins from a swimming-pool near by, when Simon came home from his office.

'I'm glad Jennie's out,' he said, 'for I wanted a chance to talk to you. I hope you won't mind,' he said, 'but Jennie's got a horror of mice.'

'Mice?' I said.

'Yes,' said Simon, 'so don't eat biscuits in your room if you wouldn't mind. Jennie was rather upset when she saw the crumbs but of course she'd have a fit if she knew I'd told you. She'd die rather than tell you. But there it is, and I know you'll understand.'

'But Jennie put the biscuits in my room herself,' I explained. 'She packed them in a box and took them up last night.'

Simon looked worried. 'We've had mice before,' he said, 'and she can't bear the thought of them upstairs.'

'Jennie put the biscuits there,' I insisted, feeling all in the wrong. 'And,' I said, 'I saw Jennie pack the box. I'll ask her about it.'

'*Please*,' said Simon, 'please don't do that. She would be so hurt to think I'd spoken about it. Please,' he said, 'go on eating biscuits in your room; I shouldn't have mentioned it.'

Of course I promised not to eat any more of the things. And Simon, with a knowing smile, said he would give me larger helpings at dinner, so that I wouldn't go hungry.

The biscuit-box had gone when I went to my room. Jennie was busy all next day preparing for a cocktail party they were giving that night. The twins devotedly gave up their day to the cutting of sandwiches and the making of curious patterns with small pieces of anchovy on diminutive squares of toast.

Jennie wanted some provisions from the village, and I offered to fetch them. I took the car, and noticed it was almost out of petrol; I got some on the way. When I returned these good children were eating their supper standing up in the kitchen, and without a word of protest, cleared off to bed before the guests arrived.

When Simon came home I met him in the hall. He was uneasy about the gin; he thought there might not be enough. He decided to go straight to the local and get more.

'And,' he said, 'I've just remembered. The car's almost out of petrol. I promised to drive the Rawlings home after the party. I nearly forgot. I'll get some petrol too.'

'Oh, I got some today,' I said.

10

There were ten guests, four married couples and two unattached girls. Jennie and I did the handing round of snacks and Simon did the drinks. His speciality was a cocktail he had just discovered, called Loopamp. This Loopamp required him to make frequent excursions to the kitchen for replenishments of prune-juice and ice. Simon persuaded himself that Loopamp was in great demand among the guests. We all drank it obligingly. As he took his shakers to the kitchen for the fourth time, he called out to one of the unattached girls who was standing by the door, 'Mollie, bring that lemon-jug too, will you?'

Mollie followed him with the lemon-jug.

'Very good scholarships,' Jennie was saying to an elderly man. 'Jeff came fourth among the boys, and Marjie took eleventh place in the girls. There were only fourteen scholarships, so she was lucky. If it hadn't been for the geography she'd have been near the top. Her English teacher told me.'

'Really!' said the man.

'Yes,' said Jennie. 'Mollie Thomas; you know Mollie Thomas. That's Marjie's English mistress. She's here tonight. Where's Mollie?' said Jennie, looking round.

'She's in the kitchen,' I said.

'Making Loopamp, I expect,' said Jennie. 'What a name, Loopamp!'

Simon and Jennie looked rather jaded the next morning. I put it down to the Loopamp. They had very little to say, and when Simon had left for London, I asked Jennie how she was feeling.

'Not too good,' she said. 'Not too good. I am really sorry, my dear, about the petrol. I wish you had asked me for the money. Now, here it is, and don't say another word. Simon's so touchy.'

'Touchy?'

'Well,' said Jennie; 'you know what men are like. I wish you had come to me about it. You know how scrupulous I am about debts. And so is Simon. He just didn't know you had got the petrol, and, of course, he couldn't understand why you felt hurt.'

I sent myself a wire that morning, summoning myself back to London. There wasn't a train before the six-thirty, but I caught this. Simon arrived home as I was getting into the taxi, and he joined Jennie and the children on the doorstep to wave goodbye.

'Mind you come again soon,' said Jennie.

As I waved back, I noticed that the twins, who were waving to me, were not looking at me, but at their parents. There was an expression on their faces which I have only seen once before. That was at the Royal Academy, when I saw a famous portrait-painter standing bemused, giving a remarkable long look at the work of his own hands. So, with wonder, pride and bewilderment, did the twins gaze upon Jennie and Simon.

I wrote and thanked them, avoiding any reference to future meetings. By return I had a letter from Simon, 'I am sorry,' he wrote, 'that you got the impression that Mollie and I were behaving improperly in the kitchen on the night of our party. Jennie was very upset. She does not, of course, doubt my fidelity, but she is distressed that you could suggest such a thing. It was very embarrassing for Jennie to hear it in front of all her friends, and I hope, for Jennie's sake, you will not mention to her that I have written you about it. Jennie would rather die than hurt your feelings. Yours ever, Simon Reeves.'

ROBERT BURNS

Auld Lang Syne

Should auld acquaintance be forgot,
    And never brought to mind?
Should auld acquaintance be forgot,
    And auld lang syne?

For auld lang syne, my dear,
    For auld lang syne,
We'll tak a cup o' kindness yet
    For auld lang syne.

And surely ye'll be your pint-stowp,
    And surely I'll be mine
And we'll tak' a cup o' kindness yet,
    For auld lang syne.

    For auld lang syne, etc.

We twa hae run about the braes,
    And pu'd the gowans fine,
But we've wander'd monie a weary fit
    Sin' auld lang syne.

    For auld lang syne, etc.

We twa hae paidl'd in the burn
   Frae morning sun til dine,
But seas between us braid hae roar'd
   Sin' auld lang syne.

   For auld lang syne, etc.

And there's a hand, my trusty fiere,
   And gie's a hand o' thine,
And we'll tak a right guid-willie waught
   For auld lang syne.

   For auld lang syne, etc.

WALTER DE LA MARE

Miss Duveen

I seldom had the company of children in my grandmother's house beside the River Wandle. The house was old and ugly. But its river was lovely and youthful even although it had flowed on for ever, it seemed, between its green banks of osier and alder. So it was no great misfortune perhaps that I heard more talking of its waters than of any human tongue. For my grandmother found no particular pleasure in my company. How should she? My father and mother had married (and died) against her will, and there was nothing in me of those charms which, in fiction at any rate, swiftly soften a super-annuated heart.

Nor did I pine for her company either. I kept out of it as much as possible.

It so happened that she was accustomed to sit with her back to the window of the room which she usually occupied, her grey old indifferent face looking inwards. Whenever necessary, I would steal close up under it, and if I could see there her large faded amethyst velvet cap I knew I was safe from interruption. Sometimes I would take a slice or two of currant bread or (if I could get it) a jam tart or a cheese cake, and eat it under a twisted old damson tree or beside the running water. And if I conversed with anybody, it would be with myself or with my small victims of the chase.

Not that I was an exceptionally cruel boy; though if I had lived on for many years in this primitive and companionless

15

fashion, I should surely have become an idiot. As a matter of fact, I was unaware even that I was ridiculously old-fashioned – manners, clothes, notions, everything. My grandmother never troubled to tell me so, nor did she care. And the servants were a race apart. So I was left pretty much to my own devices. What wonder, then, if I at first accepted with genuine avidity the acquaintanceship of our remarkable neighbour, Miss Duveen?

It had been, indeed, quite an advent in our uneventful routine when that somewhat dubious household moved into Willowlea, a brown brick edifice, even uglier than our own, which had been long vacant, and whose sloping garden confronted ours across the Wandle. My grandmother, on her part, at once discovered that any kind of intimacy with its inmates was not much to be desired. While I, on mine, was compelled to resign myself to the loss of the Willowlea garden as a kind of no man's land or Tom Tiddler's ground.

I got to know Miss Duveen by sight long before we actually became friends. I used frequently to watch her wandering in her long garden. And even then I noticed how odd were her methods of gardening. She would dig up a root or carry off a potted plant from one to another overgrown bed with an almost animal-like resolution; and a few minutes afterwards I would see her restoring it to the place from which it had come. Now and again she would stand perfectly still, like a scarecrow, as if she had completely forgotten what she was at.

Miss Coppin, too, I descried sometimes. But I never more than glanced at her, for fear that even at that distance the too fixed attention of my eyes might bring hers to bear upon me. She was a smallish woman, inclined to be fat, and with a peculiar waddling gait. She invariably appeared to be angry with Miss Duveen, and would talk to her as one might talk to a post. I did not know, indeed, until one day Miss Duveen waved her handkerchief in my direction that I had been observed from Willowlea at all. Once or twice after

16

that, I fancied, she called me; at least her lips moved; but I could not distinguish what she said. And I was naturally a litle backward in making new friends. Still I grew accustomed to looking out for her and remember distinctly how first we met.

It was raining, the raindrops falling softly into the unrippled water, making their great circles, and tapping on the motionless leaves above my head where I sat in shelter on the bank. But the sun was shining whitely from behind a thin fleece of cloud, when Miss Duveen suddenly peeped in at me out of the greenery, the thin silver light upon her face, and eyed me sitting there, for all the world as if she were a blackbird and I a snail. I scrambled up hastily with the intention of retreating into my own domain, but the peculiar grimace she made at me fixed me where I was.

'Ah,' she said, with a little masculine laugh. 'So this is the young gentleman, the bold, gallant young gentleman. And what might be his name?'

I replied rather distantly that my name was Arthur.

'Arthur, to be sure!' she repeated, with extraordinary geniality, and again, 'Arthur,' as if in the strictest confidence.

'I know you, Arthur, very well indeed. I have looked, I have watched; and now, please God, we need never be estranged.' And she tapped her brow and breast, making the sign of the cross with her lean, bluish forefinger.

'What is a little brawling brook,' she went on, 'to friends like you and me?' She gathered up her tiny countenance once more into an incredible grimace of friendliness; and I smiled as amicably as I could in return. There was a pause in this one-sided conversation. She seemed to be listening, and her lips moved, though I caught no sound. In my uneasiness I was just about to turn stealthily away, when she poked forward again.

'Yes, yes, I know you quite intimately, Arthur. We have met *here*.' She tapped her rounded forehead. 'You might not suppose it, too; but I have eyes like a lynx. It is no

17

exaggeration, I assure you – I assure everybody. And now what friends we will be! At times,' – she stepped out of her hiding-place and stood in curious dignity beside the water, her hands folded in front of her on her black pleated silk apron – 'at times, dear child, I long for company – earthly company.' She glanced furtively about her. 'But I must restrain my longings; and you will, of course, understand that I do not complain. *He* knows best. And my dear cousin, Miss Coppin – she too knows best. She does not consider too much companionship expedient for me.' She glanced in some perplexity into the smoothly swirling water.

'I, you know,' she said suddenly, raising her little piercing eyes to mine, 'I am Miss Duveen, that's not, they say, quite the thing here.' She tapped her small forehead again beneath its sleek curves of greying hair, and made a long narrow mouth at me. 'Though, of course,' she added, 'we do not tell *her* so. No!'

And I, too, nodded my head in instinctive and absorbed imitation. Miss Duveen laughed gaily. 'He understands, he understands!' she cried, as if to many listeners. 'Oh, what a joy it is in this world, Arthur, to be understood. Now tell me,' she continued with immense nicety, 'tell me, how's your dear mamma?'

I shook my head.

'Ah,' she cried, 'I see, I see; Arthur has no mamma. We will not refer to it. No father, either?'

I shook my head again and, standing perfectly still, stared at my new acquaintance with vacuous curiosity. She gazed at me with equal concentration, as if she were endeavouring to keep the very thought of my presence in her mind.

'It is sad to have no father,' she continued rapidly, half closing her eyes; 'no head, no guide, no stay, no stronghold; but we have, O yes, we have another father, dear child, another father – eh? . . . Where . . . Where?'

She very softly raised her finger. 'On high,' she whispered with extraordinary intensity.

'But just now,' she added cheerfully, hugging her

18

mittened hands together, 'we are not talking of Him; we are talking of ourselves, just you and me, *so* cosy; so *secret*! And it's a grandmother? I thought so, I thought so, a grandmother! O yes, I can peep between the curtains, though they do lock the door. A grandmother – I thought so; that very droll old lady! *Such* fine clothes! Such a presence, oh yes! A grandmother.' She poked out her chin and laughed confidentially.

'And the long, bony creature, all rub and double,' – she jogged briskly with her elbows – 'who's that?'

'Mrs Pridgett,' I said.

'There, there,' she whispered breathlessly, gazing widely about her. 'Think of that! *He* knows; *He* understands. How firm, how manly, how undaunted! . . . *One* t?'

I shook my head dubiously.

'Why should he?' she cried scornfully. 'But between ourselves, Arthur, that is a thing we *must* learn, and never mind the headache. We cannot, of course, know everything. Even Miss Coppin does not know everything' – she leaned forward with intense earnestness – 'though I don't tell her so. We must try to learn all we can; and at once. One thing, dear child, you may be astonished to hear, I learned only yesterday, and that is how exceedingly *sad* life is.'

She leaned her chin upon her narrow bosom pursing her lips. 'And yet you know they say very little about it . . . They don't *mention* it. Every moment, every hour, every day, every year – one, two, three, four, five, seven, ten,' she paused, frowned, 'and so on. Sadder and sadder. Why? Why? It's strange, but oh, so true. You really can have no notion, child, how very sad I am myself at times. In the evening, when they all gather together, in their white raiment, up and up and up, I sit on the garden seat, on Miss Coppin's garden seat, and precisely in the middle (you'll be kind enough to remember that?) and my *thoughts* make me sad.' She narrowed her eyes and shoulders. 'Yes and frightened, my child! Why must I be so guarded? One angel – the greatest *fool* could see the wisdom of that. But billions! – with their fixed eyes shining, so very boldly on me. I never prayed for so many, dear friend. And we pray for a good many odd things, you and I, I'll be bound. But there, you see, poor Miss Duveen's on her theology again – scamper, scamper, scamper. In the congregations of the wicked we must be cautious! . . . Mrs Partridge and grand-mamma, so nice, *so* nice; but even that, too, a *little* sad, eh?' She leaned her head questioningly, like a starving bird in the snow.

I smiled, not knowing what else she expected of me; and her face became instantly grave and set.

'He's right; perfectly right. We must speak evil of *no* one. *No* one. We must shut our mouths. We—' She stopped suddenly and, taking a step, leaned over the water towards me, with eyebrows raised high above her tiny face. 'S–sh!' she whispered, laying a long forefinger on her lips. 'Eavesdroppers!' she smoothed her skirts, straightened her cap, and left me; only a moment after to poke out her head at me again from between the leafy bushes. 'An assignation, no!' she said firmly, then gathered her poor, cheerful, forlorn, crooked, lovable face into a most wonder-ful contraction at me, that assuredly meant,— 'But, *yes!*'

Indeed it was an assignation, the first of how many, and how few. Sometimes Miss Duveen would sit beside me, apparently so lost in thought that I was clean forgotten. And yet I half fancied it was often nothing but feigning. Once she stared me blankly out of countenance when I ventured to take the initiative and to call out good morning to her across the water. On this occasion she completed my consternation with a sudden, angry grimace – con-tempt, jealousy, outrage.

But often we met like old friends and talked. It was a novel but not always welcome diversion for me in the long shady garden that was my privy universe. Where our alders met, mingling their branches across the flowing water, and the kingfisher might be seen – there was our usual tryst. But, occasionally, at her invitation, I would venture across the stepping-stones into her demesne; and occasionally, but very seldom indeed, she would venture into mine. How plainly I see her, tip-toeing from stone to stone, in an extraordinary concentration of mind – her mulberry petticoats, her white stockings, her loose spring-side boots. And when at last she stood beside me, her mittened hand on her breast, she would laugh on in a kind of paroxysm until the tears stood in her eyes, and she grew faint with breathlessness.

'In all danger,' she told me once, 'I hold my breath and shut my eyes. And if I could tell you of every danger, I think, perhaps, you would understand – dear Miss Coppin . . .' I did not, and yet, perhaps, very vaguely I did see the connection in this rambling statement.

Like most children, I liked best to hear Miss Duveen talk about her own childhood. I contrived somehow to discover that if we sat near flowers or under boughs in blossom, her talk would generally steal round to that. Then she would chatter on and on: of the white sunny rambling house, somewhere, nowhere – it saddened and confused her if I asked where – in which she had spent her first happy years; where her father used to ride on a black horse; and her mother to walk with her in the garden in a crinolined gown and a locket with the painted miniature of a 'divine' nobleman inside it. How very far away these pictures seemed!

It was as if she herself had shrunken back into this distant past, and was babbling on like a child again, already a little isolated by her tiny infirmity.

'That was before—' she would begin to explain precisely, and then a criss-cross many-wrinkled frown would net her rounded forehead, and cloud her eyes. Time might baffle her, but then time often baffled me too. Any talk about her mother usually reminded her of an elder sister, Caroline. 'My sister, Caroline,' she would repeat as if by rote, 'you may not be aware, Arthur, was afterwards Mrs Bute. *So* charming, *so* exquisite, *so* accomplished. And Colonel Bute

– an officer and a gentleman, I grant. And yet . . . But no! My dear sister was *not* happy. And so it was no doubt a blessing in disguise that by an unfortunate accident she was found *drowned*. In a lake, you will understand, not a mere shallow noisy brook. This is one of my private sorrows, which, of course, your grandmamma would be horrified to hear – horrified; and which, of course, Partridge has not the privilege of birth even to be informed of – *our* secret, dear child – with all her beautiful hair, and her elegant feet, and her eyes no more ajar than this; but blue, blue as the forget-me-not. When the time comes, Miss Coppin will close my own eyes, I hope and trust. Death, dear, dear child, I know they *say* is only sleeping. Yet I hope and trust *that*. To be sleeping wide awake; oh no!' she abruptly turned her small untidy head away.

'But didn't they shut *hers?*' I enquired.

Miss Duveen ignored the question. 'I am not uttering one word of blame,' she went on rapidly; 'I am perfectly aware that such things confuse me. Miss Coppin tells me not to think. She tells me that I can have no opinions worth the mention. She says, "Shut up your mouth." I must keep silence then. All that I am merely trying to express to you, Arthur, knowing you will regard it as sacred between us – all I am expressing is that my dear sister, Caroline, was a gifted and beautiful creature with not a shadow or vestige or tinge or taint of confusion in her mind. *Nothing*. And yet, when they dragged her out of the water and laid her there on the bank, looking—' She stooped herself double in a sudden dreadful fit of gasping, and I feared for an instant she was about to die.

'No, no, no,' she cried, rocking herself to and fro, 'you shall *not* paint such a picture in his young, innocent mind. You *shall* not.'

I sat on my stone, watching her, feeling excessively uncomfortable. 'But what *did* she look like, Miss Duveen?' I pressed forward to ask at last.

'No, no, no,' she cried again. 'Cast him out, cast him out. *Retro Sathanas!* We must not even *ask* to understand. My father and my dear mother, I do not doubt, have spoken for Caroline. Even I, if I must be called on, will strive to collect my thoughts. And that is precisely where a friend, you, Arthur, would be so precious; to know that you too, in your innocence, will be helping me to collect my thoughts on that day, to save our dear Caroline from Everlasting Anger. That, that! Oh dear: oh dear!' She turned on me a face I should scarcely have recognized, lifting herself trembling to her feet, and hurried away.

Sometimes it was not Miss Duveen that was a child again, but I that had grown up. 'Had now you been your handsome father – and I see him, O, so plainly, dear child – had you been your father, then I must, of course, have kept to the house . . . I must have; it is a rule of conduct, and everything depends on them. Where would Society be *else?*' she cried, with an unanswerable blaze of intelligence. 'I find, too, dear Arthur, that they increase – the rules increase. I try to remember them. My dear cousin, Miss Coppin, knows them all. But I – I think sometimes one's *memory* is a little treacherous. And then it must vex people.'

She gazed penetratingly at me for an answer that did not come. Mute as a fish though I might be, I suppose it was something of a comfort to her to talk to me.

And to suppose that is *my* one small crumb of comfort when I reflect on the kind of friendship I managed to bestow.

I actually met Miss Coppin once; but we did not speak. I had, in fact, gone to tea with Miss Duveen. The project had been discussed as 'quite, quite impossible, dear child' for weeks. 'You must never mention it again.' As a matter of fact I had never mentioned it at all. But one day – possibly when their charge had been less difficult and exacting, one day Miss Coppin and her gaunt maid-servant and companion really did go out together, leaving Miss Duveen alone in Willowlea. It was the crowning opportunity of our friendship. The moment I espied her issuing from

23

the house, I guessed her errand. She came hastening down to the waterside, attired in clothes of a colour and fashion I had never seen her wearing before, her dark eyes shining in her head, her hand trembling with excitement.

It was a still, warm afternoon, with sweet williams and linden and stocks scenting the air, when, with some little trepidation, I must confess, I followed her in formal dignity up the unfamiliar path towards the house. I know not which of our hearts beat the quicker, whose eyes cast the most furtive glances about us. My friend's cheeks were brightest mauve. She wore a large silver locket on a ribbon; and I followed her up the faded green stairs, beneath the dark pictures, to her small, stuffy bedroom under the roof. We humans, they say, are enveloped in a kind of aura; to which the vast majority of us are certainly entirely insensitive. Nevertheless, there was an air, an atmosphere as of the smell of pears in this small attic room – well, every bird, I suppose, haunts with its presence its customary cage.

'This,' she said, acknowledging the bed, the looking-glass, the deal washstand, 'this, dear child, you will pardon; in fact, you will not see. How could we sit, friends as we are, in the congregation of strangers?'

I hardly know why, but that favourite word of Miss Duveen's, 'congregation', brought up before me with extreme aversion all the hostile hardness and suspicion concentrated in Miss Coppin and Ann. I stared at the queer tea things in a vain effort not to be aware of the rest of Miss Duveen's private belongings.

Somehow or other she had managed to procure for me a bun – a saffron bun. There was a dish of a grey pudding and a plate of raspberries that I could not help suspecting (and, I am ashamed to say, with aggrieved astonishment) she must have herself gathered that morning from my grandmother's canes. We did not talk very much. Her heart gave her pain. And her face showed how hot and absorbed and dismayed she was over her foolhardy entertainment. But I sipped my milk and water, sitting on a black bandbox,

24

and she on an old cane chair. And we were almost formal and distant to one another, with little smiles and curtseys over our cups, and polished agreement about the weather.

'And you'll strive not to be sick, dear child,' she implored me suddenly, while I was nibbling my way slowly through the bun. But it was not until rumours of the tremendous fact of Miss Coppin's early and unforeseen return had been borne in on us that Miss Duveen lost all presence of mind. She burst into tears; seized and kissed repeatedly my sticky hands; implored me to be discreet; implored me to be gone; implored me to retain her in my affections, 'as you love your poor dear mother, Arthur,' and I left her on her knees, her locket pressed to her bosom.

Miss Coppin was, I think, unusually astonished to see a small strange boy walk softly past her bedroom door, within which she sat, with purple face, her hat strings dangling, taking off her boots. Ann, I am thankful to say, I did not encounter. But when I was safely out in the garden in the afternoon sunshine, the boldness and the romance of this sally completely deserted me. I ran like a hare down the alien path, leapt from stone to stone across the river; nor paused in my flight until I was safe in my own bedroom, and had – how odd is childhood – washed my face and entirely changed my clothes.

My grandmother, when I appeared at her tea-table, glanced at me now and again rather profoundly and inquisitively, but the actual question hovering in her mind remained unuttered.

It was many days before we met again, my friend and I. She had, I gathered from many mysterious nods and shrugs, been more or less confined to her bedroom ever since our escapade, and looked dulled and anxious; her small face was even a little more vacant in repose than usual. Even this meeting, too, was full of alarms; for in the midst of our talk, by mere chance or caprice, my grandmother took a walk in the garden that afternoon, and discovered us under our damson tree. She bowed in her dignified, aged way. And Miss Duveen, with her cheeks and forehead the colour of her petticoat, elaborately curtseyed.

'Beautiful, very beautiful weather,' said my grandmother.

'It is indeed,' said my friend, fixedly.

'I trust you are keeping pretty well?'

'As far, ma'am, as God and a little weakness of the heart permit,' said Miss Duveen. 'He knows all,' she added, firmly.

My grandmother stood silent a moment.

'Indeed He does,' she replied politely.

'And that's the difficulty,' ventured Miss Duveen, in her odd, furtive, friendly fashion.

My grandmother opened her eyes, smiled pleasantly, paused, glanced remotely at me, and, with another exchange of courtesies, Miss Duveen and I were left alone once more. But it was a grave and saddened friend I now sat beside.

'You see, Arthur, all bad things, we know, are best for us. Motives included. That comforts me. But my heart is sadly fluttered. Not that I fear or would shun society; but perhaps your grandmother . . . I never had the power to treat my fellow-creatures as if they were stocks and stones. And the effort not to notice it distresses me. A little hartshorn might relieve the *palpitation*, of course; but Miss Coppin keeps all keys. It is this shouting that makes civility such a task.'

'This shouting' – very faintly then I caught her meaning, but I was in no mood to sympathize. My grandmother's one round-eyed expressionless glance at me had been singularly disconcerting. And it was only apprehension of her questions that kept me from beating a retreat. So we sat on, Miss Duveen and I, in the shade, the day drawing towards evening, and presently we walked down to the waterside, and under the colours of sunset I flung in my crumbs to the minnows, as she talked ceaselessly on.

'And yet,' she concluded, after how involved a monologue, 'and yet, Arthur, I feel it is for your forgiveness I should be pleading. So much to do; such an arch of beautiful things might have been my gift to you. It is here,' she said, touching her forehead. 'I do not think, perhaps, that all I might say would be for your good. I must be silent and discreet about much. I must not provoke' – she lifted her mittened finger, and raised her eyes – 'Them,' she said gravely. 'I am tempted, terrified, persecuted. Whispering, wrangling, shouting: the flesh is a grievous burden, Arthur; I long for peace. Only to flee away and be at rest! But,' she nodded, and glanced over her shoulder, 'about much – great trials, sad entanglements, about much the Others say, I must keep silence. It would only alarm your innocence. And that I will never, *never* do. Your father, a noble, gallant gentleman of the world, would have understood my difficulties. But he is dead . . . Whatever that may mean. I have repeated it so often when Miss Coppin thought that I was not – dead, dead, dead, dead. But I don't think that even now I grasp the meaning of the word. Of you, dear child, I will never say it. You have been life itself to me.'

How generously, how tenderly she smiled on me from her perplexed, sorrowful eyes.

'You have all the world before you, all the world. How splendid it is to be a Man. For my part I have sometimes thought, though they do not of course intend to injure me, yet I fancy, sometimes, they have grudged me *my* part in it a little. Though God forbid but Heaven's best.'

She raised that peering, dark, remote gaze to my face, and her head was trembling again. 'They are saying now to one another – "*Where is she? Where is she? It's nearly dark, m'm, where is she?*" O, Arthur, but there shall be no night *there*. We must believe it, we must – in spite, dear friend, of a weak horror of glare. My cousin, Miss Coppin, does not approve of my wishes. Gas, gas, gas, all over the house, and when it is not singing, it roars. You would suppose I might be trusted with but just my own one bracket. But no – Ann, I think – indeed I fear, sometimes, has no—' She started violently and shook her tiny head. 'When I am gone,' she continued disjointedly, 'you will be prudent, cautious, dear child? Consult only your heart about me. Older you must be . . . Yes, certainly, he must be older,' she repeated vaguely. 'Everything goes on and on – and round!' She seemed astonished, as if at a sudden radiance cast on an old and protracted perplexity.

'About your soul, dear child,' she said to me once, touching my hand, 'I have never spoken. Perhaps it was one of my first duties to keep on speaking to you about your soul. I mention it now in case they should rebuke me when I make my appearance there. It is a burden; and I have so many burdens, as well as pain. And at times I cannot think very far. I *see* the thought; but it won't alter. It comes back, just like a sheep – "*Ba-aa-ah*", like that!' She burst out laughing, twisting her head to look at me the while. 'Miss Coppin, of course, has no difficulty; gentlemen have no difficulty. And this shall be the occasion of another of our little confidences. We are discreet?' She bent her head and scanned my face. 'Here,' she tapped her bosom, 'I bear his image. My only dear one's. And if you would kindly turn your head, dear child, perhaps I could pull him out.'

It was the miniature of a young, languid, fastidious-looking officer which she showed me – threaded on dingy tape, in its tarnished locket.

'Miss Coppin, in great generosity, has left me this,' she said, polishing the glass on her knee, 'though I am forbidden to wear it. For you see, Arthur, it is a duty not to brood on the past, and even perhaps, indelicate. Some day, it may be, you, too, will love a gentle girl. I beseech you, keep your heart pure and true. This one could not. Not a single word of blame escapes me. I own to my Maker, *never* to anyone else, it has not eased my little difficulty. But it is not for us to judge. Whose office is that, eh?' And again, that lean small forefinger, beneath an indescribable grimace, pointed gently, deliberately, from her lap upward. 'Pray, pray,' she added, very violently, 'pray, till the blood streams down your face! Pray, but rebuke not. They all whisper about it. Among themselves,' she added, peering out beneath and

28

between the interlacing branches. 'But I simulate inatten-tion, I simulate . . .' The very phrase seemed to have hopelessly confused her. Again, as so often now, that glassy fear came into her eyes; her foot tapped on the gravel.

'Arthur,' she cried suddenly, taking my hand tightly in her lap, 'you have been my refuge in a time of trouble. You will never know it, child. My refuge, and my peace. We shall seldom meet now. All are opposed. They repeat it in their looks. The autumn will divide us; and then, winter; but, I think, no spring. It is so, Arthur, there is a stir; and then they will hunt me out.' Her eyes gleamed again, far and small and black in the dusky pallor of her face.

It was indeed already autumn; the air golden and still. The leaves were beginning to fall. The late fruits were well-nigh over. Robins and tits seemed our only birds now. Rain came in floods. The Wandle took sound and volume, sweeping deep above our stepping stones. Very seldom after this I even so much as saw our neighbour. But I chanced on her again one still afternoon, standing fixedly by the brawling stream, in a rusty-looking, old-fashioned cloak, her scanty hair pushed high up on her forehead.

She stared at me for a moment or two, and then, with a scared look over her shoulder, threw me a little letter, shaped like a cock-hat, and weighted with a pebble stone, across the stream. She whispered earnestly and rapidly at me over the water. But I could not catch a single word she said, and failed to decipher her close spidery handwriting. No doubt I was too shy, or too ashamed, or in a vague fashion too loyal, to show it to my grandmother. It is not now a flattering keepsake. I called out loudly I must go in; and still see her gazing after me, with a puzzled, mournful expression on the face peering out of the cloak.

Even after that we sometimes waved to one another across the water, but never if by hiding myself I could evade her in time. The distance seemed to confuse her, and quite silenced me. I began to see we were ridiculous friends, especially as she came now in ever dingier and absurder clothes. She even looked hungry, and not quite clean, as well as ill; and she talked more to her phantoms than to me when once we met.

The first ice was in the garden. The trees stood bare beneath a pale blue sunny sky, and I was standing at the window, looking out at the hoar frost, when my grandmother told me that it was unlikely that I should ever see our neighbour again.

I stood where I was, without turning round, gazing out of the window at the motionless ghostly trees, and the few birds in forlorn unease.

'Is she dead, then?' I enquired.

'I am told,' was the reply, 'that her friends have been compelled to have her put away. No doubt, it was the proper course. It should have been done earlier. But it is not our affair, you are to understand. And, poor creature, perhaps death would have been a happier, a more merciful release. She was sadly afflicted.'

I said nothing, and continued to stare out of the window.

But I know now that the news, in spite of a vague sorrow, greatly relieved me. I should be at ease in the garden again, came the thought – no longer fear to look ridiculous and grow hot when our neighbour was mentioned, or be saddled with her company beside the stream.

MARION ANGUS

'Alas! Poor Queen'

She was skilled in music and the dance
And the old arts of love
At the court of the poisoned rose
And the perfumed glove,
And gave her beautiful hand
To the pale Dauphin
A triple crown to win –
And she loved little dogs
    And parrots
  And red-legged partridges
And the golden fishes of the Duc de Guise
And a pigeon with a blue ruff
She had from Monsieur d'Elboeuf.

Master John Knox was no friend to her;
She spoke him soft and kind,
Her honeyed words were Satan's lure
The unwary soul to bind.
'Good sir, doth a lissom shape
And a comely face
Offend your God His Grace
Whose Wisdom maketh these
Golden fishes of the Duc de Guise?'
She rode through Liddesdale with a song;
'Ye streams so wondrous strang,

Oh, mak' me a wrack as I come back
But spare me as I gang.'
While a hill-bird cried and cried
Like a spirit lost
By the grey storm-wind tost.

Consider the way she had to go,
Think of the hungry snare,
The net she herself had woven,
Aware or unaware,
Of the dancing feet grown still,
The blinded eyes –
Queens should be cold and wise,
And she loved little things,
     Parrots
   And red-legged partridges
And the golden fishes of the Duc de Guise
And the pigeon with the blue ruff
She had from Monsieur d'Elboeuf.

LIZ LOCHHEAD

Meeting Norma Nimmo

Hello, hello, it is you, isn't it?

I thought it was.

My, I haven't seen you since school. I have not clepped eyes on you since the Sixth Year Leavers' Social. I mind of you diving around in bleck tights and a big fisherman's jumper shoogling up esperins in Coca-Cola and eating the insides of Vick inhalers trying to get stoned.

You've not changed.

Not really, well, putting on the beef a bit but who hasnae!

Listen . . . listen, do you mind Joyce Kirdie? Mind, reddish hair, freckles, was always a hoot in the French class, did dentistry?

She killed herself.

No, no epperently she wasn't depressed. No, I asked her sister at the funeral, but no, it's a mystery . . . Order in for Liberty curtains, booked up for three weeks in the nice bit of Ibeetha, own Lawrence-home in Kirkie, rubber tube on the exhaust of her H-reg and hallelujah.

Her mother was devastated. Looked about one hundred and five. Mark you, I call it the coward's way out . . .

Do you know who I ren into outside the crematorium? Moira Lennox. Epperently she'd bumped into Merjorie Sneddon. You do mind Merjorie! She won the Mysie Thomson Inglis prize for Excellence in Art three years hard running but wisnae allowed to go to the Art School because her mother was a Plymouth Brethren?

EEC. Brussels. Bilingual private secretary to some big-wig, fabulous selery, she loved the lifestyle. Moira said a week later she was dead, choked on a truffle . . .

Mind you, poor Moira has been having her own share of troubles recently. Ocht, aye you do mind Moira Lennox. Big fet lassie, brilliant at *Letin*. Well, epperently she joined the Scotstoun branch of the Society of Serious Slimmers and ended up semi-enorexic.

Oh, wait till I tell you . . . Rosamund Petterson. Blondish, right sexpot, used to go out with the Glesgow Ecedemy School Ceptain . . . Modelled briefly. Then she married one of the Everage White Band. Or wis it mibbe the Marmalade? Anyhow, she emigrated with him to Bel Air, he divorced her for Rod Stewart's ex and she ended up with a drug dependency problem living with some elcoholic screen-writer who tried to strengle her to death in a drunken rage. Well, he could efford the good lawyer so he ended up getting off with the ettempted murder charge plus she lost custody of the children.

She's beck home now, running a wee knitwear-and-yarns shop in Clerkston.

Anyway I'm going out with her for a wee G. and T. on Gordie's squash night. She'll be *fes*cinated that I met you . . .

BRIGID BROPHY

from *The King of a Rainy Country*

The car was brought out to us in the Piazzale Roma. We stood beside it. Helena asked me, 'Is it all right?'

It was medium-large, a metallic silver-green. Either it had no roof, or the roof was rolled down at the back where there was a fold of canvas. It was very new: but its shape belonged to the thirties; it was a roadster.

'It's wonderful,' I said. 'The only word is ritzy.'

Helena smiled. She got into the driving seat and opened the other door for me. She stowed her handbag, a scarf and a pair of big leather gloves in the pocket beneath the dashboard. Starting the engine, she said, 'I have a passion for fast cars – and nice, homely men.'

We set off along the black, industrial road across the sea. Helena hoisted herself up in her seat and loosened the folds of her skirt. She began to drive with one hand, her elbow resting on the frame of the car. I looked at her. Her hair was flying. 'O, it's going to be a lovely day,' she said.

'Would you like something to eat?'

'Not yet. Do you.'

I took out a roll.

'It's good to get out of Venice for a bit,' Helena said. 'Although this is certainly a miserable road. But when we get to the mainland it'll be fresher.'

'It's fresher already.'

'Does Venice make you homesick?' she asked.

'Not particularly. Why?'

'O, Philip was talking – last night – you'd almost think he'd heard what Neale was saying down by the Molo.'

'I shouldn't have thought Philip had ideas like that.'

'O, it wasn't *like* that. It was just that Venice apparently makes him think of home. I thought to myself Neale would have an explanation for that.' She reached up and twisted the driving-mirror slightly. 'No, Philip was saying it got him down after a bit, always hearing Italian round him, and only half understanding it, and having to think before he asked for a box of matches. And all the newspapers, he said, written in Italian. He went on about how he'd like to buy an evening paper on a warm evening in London. And how the newspaper sellers chalked their own placards to mislead you – 'The Queen: a Surprise'. And when you buy the paper you find she's gone on her vacation, or something, just as usual. Or 'Race-horse Owner in Dock'. And you find a tiny paragraph on the back page, saying that someone who once bought a carthorse has been fined for parking it in the wrong place.'

'There are little nests of offenders,' I said. 'All round Marble Arch they put up terribly scaring posters.'

'There you are,' she said. 'You've got it, too. You're homesick.'

I laughed. 'No, I'm just susceptible to atmosphere. You and Philip between you built one up. Actually, I've no reason to think well of Marble Arch. I always remember walking round there and down Park Lane to a sort of employment place, where I had to go to get a job.'

'Didn't you like that?'

'No. I was scared silly.'

Helena nodded.

We came to the mainland.

'Well, we're out of Venice. Do you mind if we don't take the autostrada? I thought we might go on the country road. Would that be all right?'

'Yes, indeed,' I said.

I settled down, and the winding white road half hypnotized me. We turned in and out beside the deep river. Eventually I asked Helena, 'Does Venice make *you* homesick?'

It was a moment before she said, 'O, it would. If I had a home.'

'Where, actually, *do* you live?'

'O, everywhere. I have a place, you know, in England.'

'Have you? Where?'

'Cumberland. I bought it because the country was so beautiful. I bet you've never even been there.'

'No, I haven't. When are you coming to England again?'

'Sometime,' she said. 'Never. It's too cold. Part of the house is rented. I just have a bit of it, in case I wanted to go there. I have a sort of secretary-housekeeper who lives in it and takes care of things for me. And then I have a place – well, it's not mine, but it's a place I can go – in Paris. And – my ex-husband lives in Kentucky.'

We drove on.

'Let's have a cigarette,' she said. 'They're in there.' She tapped the bevelling of the dashboard. 'Would you light me one?'

I put it into her mouth.

'It's funny,' she said. 'Although it all ended so messily – and so soon – we divorced after two years – I still feel a sort of romance if I think of it. I look back on myself, you know – as a bride.'

'Yes. Of course.'

'Oh, I wasn't really the girl, you know, for tripping up the aisle looking cute in white. I was even a little taller than the groom.'

'Was he a nice homely man?' I asked.

'No. No, he wasn't. Perhaps it was the scare I got from him that put me on to nice homely men. Anyway, although I wasn't the type, I got through it all right. I gave a performance. I didn't fall over my dress or anything.' She looked out of the side of the car. 'This is Strà. Have you been to the palace here?'

'The Villa Pisani? Yes.'

'We won't stop then. I like it, though.'

'So do I.' We drove past the long stone blocks of the entrance lodge, with their twisted giant caryatids; and then along beside the stone wall, with the occasional iron gates giving us a glimpse of the deep park beyond. 'Were you married in white, after all?'

'O yes. I was married in London – didn't I tell you? I happened to be singing there, at the time. So we had all the trimmings. A June wedding.' She added, 'It rained like hell.'

'Of course it did.'

'As you say, of course it did. We came out of the church and just stood there on top of the steps, looking at it. Then we made a dash for the car. I was scared all the time the hem of my dress would get muddy on the pavement. I don't know why I was so worried, since I wasn't ever going to use it again.'

'What flowers did you have?'

'O, roses.'

'Yes, of course,' I said.

'I told them yellow, because I didn't think I was the girl for pink. But they got pink. I was mad.' She threw her cigarette out of the car. 'Now tell me about yourself.'

'About myself? What?'

'Oh, anything that comes to mind, as the psychoanalysts or psychiatrists or whatever they are say. Or no, don't do that. I'd probably get your dreams or your earliest memories, or something. I always feel sorry for the psychoanalysts. I can't think of anything more boring than people who tell you their dreams and their earliest memories.'

'Nor can I.'

'Go ahead and tell me something else, then.'

'I could tell you about Neale. And Cynthia.'

'That sounds fine, for a start.'

'I've never really wanted to tell anyone before,' I said. 'At least, I have. There was a woman who used to teach me at school. I wanted to tell her.'

'And didn't you?'

'She wouldn't – or couldn't – let me. I would have liked to be friends with her. But something held her back.'

'Some people are inhibited,' Helena said.

'Yes. She had some inhibition.'

'Well, go ahead and talk to me,' Helena said. 'I have no inhibitions.'

'O yes you have.'

'Yes I have. Go ahead and tell me all the same.'

We drove into Padua, and Helena parked the car in a square outside a restaurant. 'Isn't it a funny little town? I never know whether I really like it or not. Anyway, there are far too many bicycles.'

I pointed into the pocket under the dashboard, where there was still a paper bag full of rolls. 'We can hardly take them into the restaurant.'

'Leave them there, and let's hope somebody steals them. You didn't have much appetite.'

'I can't eat many rolls.' I didn't move from the car. 'Why do you have to come to Padua to have your photograph taken?'

'O, they want it in a hurry, to go in a catalogue or a publicity hand-out for a recording.'

'Have you made a new recording?'

'No, they're just putting some of the old ones on to long-play.' She stepped stiffly out.

'But why Padua?' I said.

'You mean why not Venice? Well, I've been to this man in Padua before – a long time ago. I don't know any of the people in Venice.'

'Do you hate having your photograph taken?'

'Yes. Let's draw our lunch out as long as we can. That'll give him time for his siesta and me time to compose myself.'

I got out of the car. 'Why do you hate it?'

'O, I don't know. Makes me self-conscious, I suppose.' She walked ahead of me, a little stridingly, into the restaurant.

We stepped along small, crowded pavements, in the sun; under arcades out of the sun but hardly cooler. Helena had to lead the way, but I was taking her, and whenever the crowds did not knock us apart she leaned on my arm. 'Incidentally,' she said, 'where do *you* live?'

'Nowhere. That's my answer to your living everywhere.'

She halted. 'Haven't you an address?' Someone pushed into us.

'It is amusing, the way you say *add*ress. Well, there's a girl called Tanya. We left our things at her flat, so I suppose that's our address.'

'Would you give it me?' Helena asked. She opened her handbag and tore a thin leaf of lined paper out of a diary or a notebook. She gave me the bag to hold, while she pressed the paper against the wall and wrote down Tanya's address. The pencil lines appeared: thick, and intermittent, like a flagged path, where the cast of the stone pushed through.

'Do you really want it, or are you just using up time?'

'I never do that,' she said quickly, 'even when I am scared. No, I thought I might want to write to you some time.'

'Good,' I said.

She folded the paper and took her handbag from me. We walked on.

'I shall have to go home soon,' I said.

'Have you got tickets?'

'Not for any particular date. But the money's running out.'

'Are you flying?'

'O no. Rail and sea. That's all the agency would give us.'

'Will you get another job, back in England?'

'I shall have to.'

'Mm,' she said. 'I shall be leaving Venice soon, too.'

'Why?'

'O, I get the urge, you know.' She led me into the photographer's. It was low-built and cramped, with a wooden lintel. Helena had to stoop as she went through. I caught sight of the small shop window as we passed it: draped in shiny, striped taffeta, with framed photographs standing about on it, portraits of young men in army uniform, and full-length pictures of first communicants, little girls in long white dresses, little boys in white suits with rosettes, standing sometimes in pairs and looking like sugar figures on the top of a wedding cake.

Inside, there was a carpeted box: a reception room. A small ornamental chair, with gilt stick-like legs, stood against the wall. The latch of the front door rang a bell as we closed it. A girl came. Helena introduced herself. The girl went to the back of the shop, and descended some stairs. Helena took out her comb and began to pull at her hair.

Stooping, the photographer himself made his way up the stairs : a short, young, rather pretty-faced man. 'Ah, I am so glad,' he said. He indicated Helena's comb. 'You have plenty time for that, downstairs.'

'O yes,' she said. She stood holding it. The photographer smiled, and stood back for her.

I took the comb from her.

'This is a friend,' she said, 'that I brought along to hold my hand.'

'Yes,' the photographer said. 'Pleased to meet you. You come down to the studio now?'

There were three stone steps down. He reached his hand out in advance of us. 'Excuse me. I light the light.' He pulled the switch down.

We were in a cellar: so I judged by the stone floor. The walls were hung with white sheets, roughly draped. At one side, a curtain on a rail stood pulled back, and I could see a dressing-table inside, with sticks of make-up lying on it.

In the middle of the floor stood a throne. The photographer indicated that Helena should sit there.

'And the friend,' he said. 'She sit down' – he pulled up

41

a wooden kitchen chair for me – 'behind the machine. Behind my back. So. Then she say something to make you smile.'

Helena and I sat down, opposite one another, separated by four or five yards.

The camera was a brown wooden box, long, old-looking, with a front that pulled out like a gas-mask. The photographer pushed it towards Helena, tipping the tripod along from one foot to another. He halted it, and pulled the black cloth over his head like a beekeeper's veil.

Helena stooped to put her handbag down beside the throne; then she picked it up again and set it on her lap. 'I don't know what to do with my bag.'

'Is all right,' the photographer said, under the black cotton. 'It doesn't matter. Just try to relax.' He came out. 'We get some background,' he said. He went round behind Helena and disappeared into the sheet hanging in front of the wall.

Helena sat stiff on the throne.

He came out again, pushing the sheet with him. He hooked it loose, and began to edge out a tall, folded screen. It was green, covered in a miniature, rather Persian-looking, pattern of leaves, branches and blossoms, with occasional blue peacocks and parrot-like birds with long tails, perching, each about three inches high.

Manoeuvring it as if it was in some way human, he got the screen into place behind Helena's throne, and opened out its wings into a semicircle.

He ran back to the camera, and under cloth again. 'Is better. Now we have some light.'

He pushed a lamp to Helena's side, adjusted its angle and turned a wheel. The stem lengthened. The tilted shade towered above the throne, the naked bulb pointing at Helena.

He switched it on.

I saw Helena's eyes water. She looked down.

The photographer came back, into the camera cloth

again. 'Don't look so sad,' he said. 'We want a happy picture. Look at your friend and laugh.'

Helena tried to look up. 'It's this damn light,' she said. 'It's like being grilled by the Communists.'

Immediately the light fizzled and went out.

The ordinary lighting of the cellar was dim by comparison.

Neatly, the photographer held his finger up to Helena. 'Uh. You said Communist to it. That is a naughty word. I get another light.'

He hurried across to the dressing-table and began pulling out the drawers. I saw electric-light bulbs rolling about in the spilt powder. He brought one out, dusted it, lowered the lamp, fitted it: he switched on: no light came. 'O-o-oh,' he said, and shrugged. 'I have to go out and get another. You excuse me? I try not to be long.'

'That's all right,' Helena said.

For a moment after his departure, she sat still on the throne. Then 'How long do you think he's gone for?' she said. 'Long enough for a cigarette?'

'Don't you think this place is full of inflammable stuff? I mean, film and photographic chemicals and so on.'

She opened her handbag. 'Let's break the rules.'

She lit our cigarettes.'

'It's rather a nice screen, isn't it?'

'I wonder what's behind it,' she said. 'Behind the curtain, I mean, where he got it from.' She got up, turned back the screen and parted the curtains. I peered round her shoulders. 'You can't see much,' I said.

She lit her cigarette lighter and held it out, between the curtains. There was a small recess, which seemed to be piled with silk and screens.

'I'm sure all this is inflammable, anyway.'

'O well,' she said, 'if we burn his shop down, we'll just have to pay for it.'

'Neale's right. You are glamorously wealthy.'

'To be as wealthy as a photographer in Padua? O, I don't

think that's aiming too high.' She pointed down at a corner of the recess. 'What's that?'

I went on to my hands and knees and crawled beneath the curtain. 'It seems to be a pillar. Or a bit of one.' Holding my cigarette in one hand, I tried to roll the pillar out. Helena held the curtain up, to give me light. 'Lift it,' she said. 'It won't be heavy.'

I tried. It was made of cardboard. I carried it out into the light and set it down near the throne. It was made to represent part of a classical column, broken off. It stood on a square base, and the fluting was painted in with grey paint. Some ivy leaves had been painted on the irregular top, trailing down one side. It was naturalistically and clumsily done; but from a distance, or beneath a strong light that cast deep shadows, it would have made its classical effect.

Helena looked at it. 'Heavens.'

She went behind the curtain again.

I touched the pillar, tilted it, tapped it. 'It's got something,' I said towards the curtains, 'simply because it is cardboard. I mean, it's not so much a thing as a motif.'

'How do you mean?' her voice said from the dark.

'O, it's a trapping. Pierrot in love with the moon.'

'Here are some real trappings for you.' Her hand came through the curtains, jangling a wreath of roses, some paper, some silk, with dark green leaves of canvas, all tangled up together. She shook them; one silk one fell on to the floor.

She tossed the others back, and picked up the fallen one.

I said, 'Why don't you have your photograph taken with it?'

'O, I'm no good for wearing flowers. I'm not feminine enough.' She held it out to me. 'You wear it.'

I took it. 'Where? Behind my ear? Between my teeth?'

'Now don't be silly,' she said.

'How repressive you can be.'

'No I'm not. But I meant you to wear it seriously.' She

44

pushed it through the lapel of my dress. 'It suits you. Leave it there.'

She sat down again on the throne, but now she leaned back, her knees apart. I rested my wrists on the column. 'You know what you said to Neale about underestimating friendship?'

'Yes?'

'I was just thinking I've never experienced it.'

'Now you're being silly again,' she said. 'I'm sure you have. I'm sure you're a very warm-hearted person.'

'No. I've been in love, or acquainted with people because I wanted to use them in some way, or I've hated them. I hated you at first.' After a pause I said, 'How odd. It was only a day or two ago that Neale was asking me to sound Philip to find out if he was your lover.'

'Did he ask you to do that?'

'Yes.'

'He's not, you know. I mean Philip isn't.'

'No, I know.'

'I reckon you were impatient with people,' Helena said. 'That's why you weren't friends with them. You wanted them to give you something, always.'

'I suppose that's it.'

'Whereas, in fact, if you don't look for it, you often get given things. Still, it's natural to be impatient when you're young.'

'I once told Neale I could stand anything but a status quo.'

'And now,' Helena said, 'one would give anything for a status quo. If only it would last. What were you and Neale really looking for?'

'A moment,' I said, 'that should be immortal. A moment to set up against those moments when you wake in the night and realize – O, that Venice will crumble into the sea one day, and that even before that you'll be dead yourself.'

Helena nodded. 'O, those moments in the night,' she said. 'When they come on me now, I just say to myself:

Well, you know now. You're going to die. That's all there is to it.'

I looked at her, smiling, over my pillar. 'O Helena, I do like you.'

'That's a good thing,' She gathered herself robustly in her chair. 'Because I like you.'

'I wonder why?'

'Why?' she said. 'O, sympathy of some sort. *Tu sei molto simpatica.*'

'Everyone is in Italy,' I said. 'It's worse than mamma. Perhaps you've seen the flaw in my personality, and your imagination has made its way in.'

'Have you seen the flaw in mine?' she asked.

'Some of it. A little crack. It's why one likes you.'

After a moment, we heard the photographer's footsteps. 'Stub out your cigarette,' Helena whispered.

He came in, carrying a paper parcel. 'I am so sorry – Ah, you have found my column. You have found my roses.'

'May we keep one of them?' Helena asked.

'But of course. Would you like us to make the picture of you with the column? You hold a rose?'

'No,' Helena said. 'Certainly not. It'll do right here.'

He fitted the new bulb and put on the light. Helena winced. 'And now – one last thing.' He approached her, and knelt at the foot of the throne. He reached up and began rouging her cheeks, filling in the hollows at the side. She moved slightly, like a dummy, under his pressure. He added some brown grease-paint to the eyebrow pencil she already wore, and she blinked as he did it.

Awkward, she sat in the throne, scowling a little against the light, while he took the pictures.

'That is all,' he said. 'I have finished.'

She got up. 'Thank God. Look, if I give you the address, could you send the proofs to me in Vienna?'

'Certainly I could.'

We walked back to the car. When we got in, Helena took her powder compact out of her handbag. 'I want to get this

46

stuff off my cheeks. You look somewhere else. I don't like to look at my face when there's anyone else there.'

I looked out of the side of the car. 'Why do you want the proofs to go to Vienna?'

'Because I'm going there. I thought I'd go and see some old friends, and then I might go on to Salzburg. I'd like to hear some Mozart well done before I die. It'll be odd to be in the audience.'

'Write and tell me about it,' I said.

'O, I will. You won't come with me? You and Neale?'

'No, I can't.'

'No, right. I'll send you a report on the music. A pretty pernickety one, I daresay. I'm hard to satisfy nowadays. I've got something else for you than that, though.'

'What?'

'A sort of present. Something I'd like you to have. Now I know your address, I can wire my housekeeper-cum-secretary and get her to send it you in London.'

'You won't say what it is?'

She started the car. 'You may have a use for it,' she said. 'Or you may not. It doesn't matter if not. Don't feel I'd mind.'

'When are you leaving for Austria?'

'Soon.' She smiled at me. 'I've driven quite far on my own today, haven't I? I reckon if I take it in easy stages, stopping, you know, at little places in the mountains, I can make it.'

'You're not going to take Philip, then?'

'No, that's part of the idea. I'm going to give Philip a rest.'

On the drive home, we stopped at Strà. We went into an inn, and had dinner in the courtyard in the evening coolness. Helena said, 'Why don't we stay the night?'

'Don't you want to drive any further?'

'Not much. Would you mind?'

'No. I could ring Neale, I suppose.'

'You do that. And I'll send this wire. I'll ask the proprietor if he has rooms.'

After we had engaged them, we went out to the car. Children were scrambling over it, Helena got in, and drove it into the courtyard of the inn. I walked after her. I got the paper bag of rolls out. 'That's all our luggage,' Helena said. 'Will you be all right?' I nodded. 'Let's find the phone,' she said.

There was a box in the hall of the hotel. Helena went in and sent her telegram. She came out and held open the door for me. I asked, 'You wouldn't get through for me, would you?'

'Surely.'

She came out again, holding the receiver towards me. I went in, and she shut the door behind me.

'Neale? Are you all right?'

'Yes, of course.'

'We're going to stay at Strà. Helena doesn't want to drive any more.'

'Yes. I don't mind.'

'We'll be back early tomorrow.'

'Well, you'll probably find me here.'

'Yes. I'll come straight to the pensione.'

'O, take your time.'

I said, 'What have you been doing all day?'

'O, wandering round. I ran into Philip and Cynthia.'

'How was her screen test?'

'No good.'

'Can they tell? So soon?'

He laughed. 'They didn't bother to look, even. Girdler just apologized and said she wasn't the sort of actress he'd thought she was.'

'O Lord. It's probably our fault.'

'I'm not taking any blame,' he said.

'I hope you were nice to her.'

'I wasn't nasty.'

'What will you do this evening?'

'Wander round, I daresay. I expect Cynthia will want to go to bed and mourn. I might have a bachelor night out with Philip.'

'Don't sound so bitter, Neale.'

'I'm not,' he said.

I told Helena about Cynthia's screen test. She shook her head.

My room was a whitewashed attic. The ceiling sloped down to a square window, with a narrow, wooden window-seat.

I lay in bed naked beneath a sheet. I could see the basin and ewer on the table. The maid had told me that all the water came from the well in the courtyard. She had brought it up, and I had washed; it was cold and pale brown.

I could see through the window the trees of the courtyard with stars behind them.

Helena came into my room. 'I'm not going to say I couldn't sleep. It just seemed too good to waste.' She sat down on the window seat. 'I had to put my dress on to come. I guess they wouldn't like me to run round the corridors with nothing on.'

She threw me a cigarette. I saw her light her own. Then she threw her lighter on to the bottom of my bed.

She leaned out of the window. 'I can smell horse dung and lime trees.'

She smoked, then stubbed her cigarette out on the window-ledge and threw it into the courtyard.

'All this about finding the moment,' she said.

'Yes?'

'There's nothing in the world but people, is there?'

'No, nothing. How do you mean?'

'Well, like what you said about imagination and sympathy. People find their way into one another's personalities. You give to one person, take from another – give and take vitality, I mean. But nobody has all the vitality. Nobody is a reservoir. It's just an exchange. It goes round in an endless cycle.'

'I suppose so,' I said.

'Just as one gets one's vitality, in the first place, from one's mother's body. Just as I should have liked to pass it on to a child of my own.'

'Yes.'

She sat for some time perfectly still. She got up, said Good night, and went.

We took the vaporetto back from the Piazzale Roma to San Marco. I saw Helena to her hotel; then I walked round to the pensione. I went up to our bedroom. The maid was just coming out, carrying a long brush; she wished me *Buon giorno*.

Neale was not there. I lay down on my bed and smoked.

He came in at about half-past eleven. He looked tired. In his lapel he was wearing the shabby silk rose which Cynthia had given me underneath the stage at school. He looked at me and said, 'Ho, you've got one too.'

'Yes. How are you?'

'Fine. Did you have fun at Strà?'

'We stayed at rather a nice place.'

'Good.'

I said, 'You look a bit worn. Did you go on the town with Philip?'

'No,' he said. Then: 'I slept with Cynthia.'

'O. I see.'

'Well?'

'Well what?' I asked. 'Are you glad about it?'

'Quite. Why shouldn't I be?'

'No reason at all. Is she glad?'

'I imagine so. I didn't ask her.'

I said, 'Where?'

'Where? O, at her hotel. It was funny, there were no difficulties at all. I just went up to her room. And came down again next day.'

'There's no point in asking why?'

'Why? O, well she was fed-up, I suppose, at not getting a job with Girdler.'

'Yes, but why did you?'

'Me? She told me to, I suppose.'

I nodded. I lit another cigarette. 'It's funny how it seems to seal two people up together, so that one's imagination can't approach them.'

'I suppose it does.'

'If you're glad about it,' I said, 'you've no reason to be ashamed with me.'

'I'm not ashamed.'

'You seem on edge. I thought you might think you'd treated me badly.'

'You? O no. I've treated you better than I've ever treated anyone.'

'Have you?'

'Yes, of course. I kept you travelling hopefully, didn't I? Isn't that the kindest thing one can do for anyone?' He walked over to the mantelpiece and played with the model châlet, opening and shutting its front door.

I said, 'You'll probably break it if you force it like that.'

'O, one can't always wait for the weather.' He turned the châlet upside down. 'Is it true that women always want to marry men they've slept with?'

I said, 'I don't know. I should think some do, some don't. It's probably as true as any of the ideas you can pick up from women's magazines. Does Cynthia want to marry you?'

'She's told me to marry her.'

'Do you mean you're going to?'

'Yes.'

'O. That does alter things.'

'Yes,' he said.

'Neale, is all this serious? I mean, it's not just one of those engagements—'

'No, quite serious. I've written to my parents.'

'*Why* are you doing it?' I said.

'Cynthia's rather tired of trying to start a career that's obviously not going to get anywhere. She'd like to settle down. And have children.'

51

'Yes, I quite see that. You'll have to get a job, I suppose? A proper job?'

'Yes. When we get back to England. I shall do what's called going into business.' He put the châlet down. 'This object embodies everything I most hate about life.'

I said, 'I wonder what life with Cynthia will be like when she hasn't even got the slight glamour of films about her.'

'Quiet, I expect,' he said. 'My quietus.'

'Neale, do you mean you've given up the search?'

He turned and smiled at me. 'O, but we were searching for Cynthia, weren't we? And now I've found her.'

'No,' I said. 'We were searching long before I told you about her.'

'But possibly *you* were searching for her,' he said, 'without knowing it.'

'No, I was searching even before I knew her at school. In fact, that's why I came to know her.'

'O well, in that case,' he said, 'yes. I have given up. Come on, let's go to lunch.'

In the trattoria, I said to him, 'Now you've sealed yourselves up in an official engagement, this is an unforgivable question. But you're not in love with her, are you?'

He smiled and hesitated. 'No. No, I'm not. But at the back of my mind I have the faintest feeling – as if I had, once, been in love with her.'

I said, 'You really have adopted my past.'

'Have I? What did you want me to adopt – your future?'

'My present.'

'Isn't it amusing of English that that should be a pun? But, you see, the things you give people really depend on what they have the power to accept. And I can only take your past.' He smiled. 'It's your wedding present.'

He paid, and we rose to go.

'I'm meeting Cynthia under the Campanile,' he said.

'O.'

'I'm taking her to the Lido. Coming?'

'No. I'll go back and lie down for a bit.'

I slept deeply for two hours. The maid woke me, coming in to turn down the beds. I told her I wouldn't be a moment; she waited outside; I saw her, and she smiled at me, as I went out.

I wandered for a little and went into a church. Someone was in the confessional, and a verger walked up and down staring at me. I came out. Although I was not lost, I panicked at finding myself alone in Venice, and I hurried to Helena's hotel. I was told both she and Philip were out. I went back to the pensione. Philip was waiting in the flowery hall. 'I've brought you a note from Helena.'

'May I open it now?'

'Yes, do. Please.' He turned aside while I read it.

Sorry to be so abrupt, but you know how it is. I'm off this afternoon. I got the wanderlust and I don't want to keep P. hanging around. I'll send you a postcard from the mountains if I get the chance, and in any case I'll write properly when I arrive. Regards to N. Best love – Helena.

'So she's off,' Philip said. 'I hope it will be all right.'

'She said she was going to friends.'

'Yes. From the old days, you know. She went in a great hurry. She'd hardly let me come down to the garage to say goodbye.' He smiled at me. 'Well, how are you? It seems a long time since I saw you. I haven't told you about Cynthia's screen test, have I?'

'I gather it was a failure.'

'She was upset, I think. Is she all right today, do you know? I haven't seen her today.'

I told him about Cynthia and Neale.

He said, 'O. Do you mind? Do you mind my asking?'

'I don't mind your asking. I do mind about Neale, rather.'

'I thought you did. I'm awfully sorry.' After a moment, he added, 'One thing I'm sure of. Helena would never have gone off just at this moment, if she'd known.'

'No, I'm sure she wouldn't,' I said. 'But I'm glad she did. I don't want to lean on her too heavily.'

'No,' he said.

The four of us had coffee together, after dinner, in the Piazza. I gave Cynthia my congratulations. She giggled slightly and said, 'Yes, it is rather exciting, isn't it?'

'Very, I should imagine.'

She smiled at me frankly. 'It's nice to be with friends, at a moment like this. Really old friends, I mean.' She glanced over the table. 'No offence, Philip. I count you as an old friend.'

'Well, old, yes,' he said, smiling. 'But I was hardly at school with you.' He said to Neale, 'What are you two – you and Cynthia – thinking of doing? I mean, will you go straight home?'

'Cynthia wants to stay on for a bit.'

'Well, now we're here,' she said. 'We might as well have a holiday. Don't you think, Philip?'

'It seems a first-rate idea.'

'One thing,' Cynthia said. 'If we can find anywhere that can take us, we'll move over to the Lido. It seems silly to have to go over there every day, and then come back again.'

Neale said to me, 'You can have the room in the pensione to yourself at last.'

'Yes,' I said. 'But I think I'll go home.'

Philip turned to me. 'Look, I've got an air ticket. A spare one, I mean. Milan London.'

'Helena's?'

'Yes. She thought she'd be going to England. I'm sure we could get it transferred to your name.'

'O no,' I said. 'You'd better sell it. The money belongs to Helena.'

'She wanted you to have the ticket. She said she knew you weren't looking forward to the journey home. She said I was to try and make you accept it.'

I asked when it was for.

'Day after tomorrow,' Philip said. 'You won't mind travelling with me?'

'No, of course—'

Neale said, 'You take it. Then Cynthia can have your railway tickets, and we can come home at our leisure.'

I said, 'All right. Thank you, Philip. It's very nice of Helena.'

'It's all fitted in very neatly,' Neale said.

'Yes,' Cynthia said, 'hasn't it?'

As we lay in our beds that night, Neale said to me, 'Shall I tell you the whole tragedy of life? By the time you find out it's mamma you want, she's too old.'

I said nothing.

'Don't you agree?' he said.

'Let's try to go to sleep.'

We circled, gently losing height. I leaned back in my chair so that Philip, straining at his safety-belt, could lean past me and look down through the window.

'At least it seems to be good weather in London,' he said.

We dropped nauseatingly.

Philip said, 'O God, I wish she could get better.'

'What do you mean?' I said.

We ran along, low above the ground. I felt a touch, a slight rebound; through the window I saw the big rubber tyres begin to spin as we landed. Philip said, 'Didn't she tell you she was dying?'

The passengers began to move, taking their coats from the rack, even before the plane stopped. I followed Philip out and across the airfield; through passport control; through the customs, where the officer questioned Philip and then marked my luggage through with his. We went out, into the bus, and found places on the upper half-deck.

'I don't know whether she told me or not.'

'I gather that whether she did or not, you didn't understand?'

'I don't know whether I understood.'

We arrived at the air terminal at Waterloo, and collected

our luggage. 'I'm going to take the tube,' Philip said. 'Are you?'

'I may as well.'

He picked up the two heaviest suitcases, one of his and one of mine, and led the way. 'Is Waterloo quite convenient for you?'

'Fairly, yes.'

'I go through on the Northern Line,' he said. 'I live in Hampstead.'

'Philip, could you lend me some money?'

'Yes, of course. How much?'

'I don't know. I was thinking. If I could get a seat on the plane I might fly to Vienna. Straight away.'

'I might come with you. Do you think she'd mind if I turned up?'

'I'm sure not.'

He carried the cases across the road and set them down on the pavement. 'We'd better go back to the air place and fix it up. I can give them a cheque.'

Outside the tube station, there were three newsvendors. On a blank sheet of paper, each had chalked himself a headline. Two were about the TUC. The third read, 'Singer Dies on Travels'.

Philip said, 'They're often misleading, you know. They do it to make you buy—'

'I know.' I felt in my handbag for two pennies.

'I'll get it,' he said. He bought the paper, and stood looking down the front page. He paused, near the bottom. 'I'm afraid it is.' He showed me a paragraph of three or four lines, saying Helena had collapsed at a country hotel in the mountains, not many miles short of Vienna; she had been taken to a hospital and had died there.

Philip asked, 'Would you like me to stay with you a bit?'

'No, not for me. Would you?'

'No, I think I'll get home, if you're all right. Are you coming on the Tube?'

'Not just now. I must ring up Tanya and see if anyone's there to let me in.'

'Can you manage your cases?'

'Yes.'

We said goodbye.

I carried my luggage into a phone box and rang Tanya. There was no reply. I walked through to the mainline station and put my cases in the left luggage office. I took the tube to Tottenham Court Road. I came out, and walked up the road past the cinemas. At the last one I came to, almost next door to the one that had been showing it when I left, *Tosca* was playing. I looked at the stills outside. A notice in the foyer said 'Last Day'. I walked back again to Oxford Street, and took a seventy-three; I sat on top and found I was pressing my fingernails into the ball of muscle at the base of my thumb. I got off at Marble Arch, went down into the tube and found an empty phone box. I looked up the number and rang my dentist.

The nurse answered.

I asked if I could have an appointment at once.

'Is it urgent? Are you in actual pain?'

'No. That's the trouble.'

'I don't quite see what you mean.'

'I haven't been for some time. There's bound to be something that needs doing, isn't there?'

'If it's just a check-up,' she said, 'I'm afraid I can't book you for at least a week. We're terribly full. I've got a space for next Friday.'

'I'll leave it. It was only an idea.'

I came out by the exit on the edge of the Park. I walked round the curve, past the bus queues. There were several newsvendors, one with the headline 'Singer Dead in Mountains'. I bought another copy of the same paper. The paragraph had been moved from the front page. I found it, curtailed, in the centre pages. I went into the Park and put the paper in a rubbish bin.

I crossed the road, walked a little way down Park Lane

and turned left. I went up to the d'Arcy Appointments Bureau. I was not quite sure that it was the same Miss d'Arcy who received me; but she said, 'Yes, I remember. Wait a moment. Didn't we fix you up with a bookseller?'

'That's right.'

'Wasn't he satisfactory?'

'He folded up.'

'O, I'm sorry to hear that. We'll have to find you something else, won't we?'

'I'd like something a bit more serious this time. Something that offers more of a career.'

She looked through her card-index box. 'You're in luck. I've actually got two publishers who want secretaries.'

She began to type. 'Aren't we having wonderful weather?'

I looked round. The room was full of sun. 'O. Yes.'

She gave me the piece of paper. 'There you are. I've never heard of the first one, I'm afraid, but the second is a very good firm. I'm sure you'd enjoy working there.'

I looked at the two addresses. The first was in EC4: the firm which published *The Lady Revealed*. I said, 'I'll try the second. I'll go along there now.'

'I hope you get fixed up all right,' she said.

I carried my luggage in from the taxi and rang Tanya's doorbell.

'Well, well, well,' she said. 'Fancy seeing you.'

'I came rather suddenly. I rang earlier but you weren't in.'

She picked up my cases, and took them through. 'Lovely to see you at any time.'

As I followed her through the hall, I saw a glossy postcard with a photograph of a mountain under snow. It lay, picture up, on the table. I turned it over. It was for me. Helena had written diagonally across the correspondence square, 'All well so far. Will write properly when I arrive.'

I followed Tanya into the bedroom.

'Well,' she said. 'I'm glad you came. I'm going away, and I didn't like to leave because I had your things. I'm all packed up, as you can see.' She pointed to the corner. Her suitcases were standing beside mine.

'I couldn't have your flat, could I?'

'Do you want it? I should think you could have it.'

'How much is it?'

'Three pounds a week.'

'I could manage that. I've just got a new job,' I said.

'Have you? There's not much room here, of course. There's only one bed.'

'O, Neale won't be coming.'

'Have you split?'

'Yes. He's getting married.'

'My poor dear. Still, you've got plenty of other fish to fry. You'll have to start looking out all those old letters you've got and ringing the boys up.'

'Yes.'

'Will you be responsible for Neale's things?' she asked. 'Will you get them back to him?'

'Yes, all right.'

'I think everything's okay. I played some of your records. Did you mind?'

'No.'

'Well, you could unpack if you'd like. I've emptied the chest of drawers.'

'Right. Thank you.'

I pulled out the deepest drawer.

'That's right,' Tanya said. 'Start at the bottom.'

I got out the box of letters and put it into the drawer. Out of my handbag I took the rose from the photographer's in Padua. I dropped it in.

'O, you've brought the rose back,' Tanya said.

'No. It's a replacement.'

'You've obviously had quite a holiday.'

I put Helena's postcard in.

'O, you got your postcard. It came yesterday. It made me wonder if you'd be home soon. Did you see the parcel?'

'What parcel?'

'I put it under the table in the hall. It came this morning. It's a bit dark in there – you probably didn't see.'

She went out and came back with a shallow oblong parcel. 'Were you expecting it?'

'Yes. It's a present.'

'Birthday? Or are you getting married too?'

'No.'

'Something for your bottom drawer, then,' Tanya said.

I knelt on the floor, with the drawer open beside me, and made no move towards the parcel. Tanya put it down on the bed. 'O well. I'll go and make some supper. If I'd known to expect you, I'd have run up something special. I'm quite good, you know,' she called from the corridor.

I pulled the parcel down and unwrapped it. Inside there was a cardboard box. I took off the lid. There was a fold of tissue paper with a card lying on it. Above the printed name 'Helena Buchan', Helena's secretary had typed the words 'with the compliments of'.

I turned back the tissue.

Inside there was something lace. At first I thought it was coffee-coloured; then I saw it was only a little faded, the effect increased by the poor light in Tanya's room.

I pulled it out. I pushed Tanya's bed to one side and spread the lace on the floor. It was a wedding dress, cut in a fashion of the late twenties or early thirties, with a square neck and no waist, and made for a woman much bigger than I was. It lay, front upward, on the floor. The front of the skirt was cut short; I guessed the white stockings must have shown, and the white buttoned shoes. The back hem protruded beyond it. Along its inside edge there was an irregular, thin band which reminded me of the shading we had used to pencil in, in geography lessons at school, to mark the coast on our maps: a narrow line, quite blanched now of any dirtiness, which showed where the bride had run across the rainy pavement towards the temporary shelter of the bridal car.

ISAAC ROSENBERG

'Break of Day In the Trenches'

The darkness crumbles away.
It is the same old druid Time as ever,
Only a live thing leaps my hand,
A queer sardonic rat,
As I pull the parapet's poppy
To stick behind my ear.
Droll rat, they would shoot you if they knew
Your cosmopolitan sympathies
(And God knows what antipathies).
Now you have touched this English hand
You will do the same to a German
Soon, no doubt, if it be your pleasure
To cross the sleeping green between.
It seems you inwardly grin as you pass
Strong eyes, fine limbs, haughty athletes,
Less chanced than you for life,
Bonds to the whims of murder,
Sprawled in the bowels of the earth,
The torn fields of France.
What do you see in our eyes
At the shrieking iron and flame
Hurled through still heavens?
What quaver – what heart aghast?
Poppies whose roots are in man's veins

Drop, and are ever dropping;
But mine in my ear is safe –
Just a little white with the dust.

ELIZABETH MCCRACKEN

from *The Giant's House*

See Also

I do not love mankind.

People think they're interesting. That's their first mistake. Every retiree you meet wants to supply you with his life story.

An example: thirty-five years ago a woman came into the library. She'd just heard about oral histories, and wanted to string one together herself.

'We have so many wonderful old people around,' she said. 'They have such wonderful stories. We could capture them on tape, then maybe transcribe them – don't you think that would make a wonderful record of the area? My father, for instance, is in a nursing home—'

Her father. Of course. She was not interested in *the* past, but *her* past.

'If I wanted to listen to old people nattering on,' I told her, 'I would ride a Greyhound bus across country. Such things get boring rather quickly, don't they?'

The woman looked at me with the same smile she'd had on the entire conversation. She laughed experimentally.

'Oh Miss Cort,' she said. 'Surely you didn't mean that.'

'I did and I do,' I answered. My reputation even thirty-five years ago was already so spoiled there was no saving it. 'I really don't see the point, do you?'

I felt that if those old people had some essential information they should write it down themselves. A life story can make adequate conversation but bad history.

Still, there you are in a nursing home, bored and lonely, and one day something different happens. Instead of a gang of school kids come to bellow Christmas carols at you, there's this earnest young person with a tape recorder, wanting to know about a flood sixty years ago, or what Main Street was like, or some such nonsense. All the other people in the home are sick to death of hearing your stories, because really let's be honest you only have a few.

Suddenly there's a microphone in your face. Wham! just like that, you're no longer a dull conversationalist, you're a natural resource.

Back then I thought, if you go around trying to rescue every fact or turn of phrase, you would never stop, you would eavesdrop until your fingers ached from playing the black keys of your tape recorder, until the batteries had gasped their last and the tape came to its end and thunked the machine off, *no more*, and still you would not have made a dent on the small talk of the world. People are always downstairs, talking without you. They gather in front of stores, run into each other at restaurants, and talk. They clump together at parties or couple up at the dinner table. They organize themselves by profession (for instance, waitresses), or by quality of looks, or by hobby, or companion (in the case of dog owners and married people), or by sexual preference or weight or social ease, and they talk.

Imagine what there is to collect: every exchange between a customer and a grocery store clerk, wrong numbers, awful baby talk to a puppy on the street, what people yell back at the radio, the sound the teenage boy outside my window makes when he catches the basketball with both his hands and his stomach, every *oh lord* said at church or in bed or standing up from a chair. *Thank you, hey watch it, gesundheit, who's a good boy, sweetness, how much? I love your dress.*

An Anthology of Common Conversation. Already I can tell you it will be incomplete. In reference works, as in sin, omission is as bad as willful misbehavior. All those words go around and end up nowhere; your fondest wishes won't save them. No need to be a packrat of palaver anyhow. Best to stick with recorded history.

Now, of course, I am as guilty as anyone, and this book is the evidence. I'm worse; I know my details by heart, no interviews necessary. No one has asked me a question yet, but I will not shut up.

Peggy Cort is crazy, anyone will tell you so. That lady who wanted to record the town's elders, the children who visited the library, my co-workers, every last soul in this town. The only person who ever thought I wasn't is dead; he is the subject of this memoir.

Let me stop. History is chronological, at least this one is. Some women become librarians because they love order; I'm one. Ordinal, cardinal, alphabetical, alphanumerical, geographical, by subject, by color, by shape, by size. Something logical that people – one hopes – cannot botch, although they will.

This isn't my story.

Let me start again.

I do not love mankind, but he was different.

He was a redhead as a child.

You won't hear that from most people. Most people won't care. But he had pretty strawberry blond hair. If he'd been out in the sun more, it would have been streaked gold.

He first came into my library in the fall of 1950, when he was eleven. Some teacher from the elementary school brought them all trooping in; I was behind the desk, putting a cart of fiction in order. I thought at first he was a second teacher, he was so much taller than the rest, tall even for a grown man. Then I noticed the chinos and white bucks and saw that this was the over-tall boy I'd heard about. Once I realized, I could see my mistake; though he would eventually develop cheek-bones and whiskers, now he was pale and slightly babyfaced. He wasn't the tallest man in the world then, just a remarkably tall boy. Doctors had not yet prescribed glasses, and he squinted at faraway objects in a heroic way, as if they were new countries waiting to be discovered.

'This is Miss Cort,' the teacher said, gesturing at me. 'Ask her any question you want. She is here to help you. That is what librarians do.'

She showed them the dusty oak card catalog, the dusty stacks, the circulation desk I spent hours keeping free of dust. In short, she terrified them.

'Fiction is on the third floor,' she said. 'And biography is on the second.' I recognized her; she read Georgette Heyer and biographies of royalty and returned books so saturated with cigarette smoke I imagined she exhaled over each page on purpose. I wanted to stand by the exit, to whisper in every eleven-year-old ear, 'Just come back. Come back by yourself and we'll forget all about this.'

At the end of the visit, the tall boy came up to talk. He seemed studious, though studious is too often the word we give to quiet odd people.

'I want a book,' he said, 'about being a magician.'

'What sort of magician?' I said. 'Like Merlin?' Recently a teacher had read aloud from *The Sword and the Stone*, and they all wanted more stories.

'No,' he said. He put his hands on the circulation desk. His fingernails were cleaner than an ordinary eleven-year-old's; his mother was then still alive. 'Just tricks,' he said. 'I want to make things look like they disappear. I looked in the card catalog under magic, but I didn't find anything.'

'Try "conjuring,"' I told him.

We found only one book, an oversized skinny volume called *Magic for Boys and Girls*. He took it to a table in the front room. He wasn't clumsy, as you might expect, but terribly delicate. His hands were large, out of proportion even with his big body, and he had to use them delicately to accomplish anything at all.

I watched his narrow back as he read the book. After an hour I walked over.

'Is that the sort of thing you wanted?' I asked.

'Yes,' he said, not looking at me. The book was opened flat on the table in front of him, and he worked his hands in the air according to the instructions, without any props. His fingers kept slowly snatching at nothing, as if he had already made dozens of things disappear, rabbits and cards and rubber balls and bouquets of paper flowers, and had done this so brilliantly even he could not bring them back.

I may be adding things. It's been years now, and nearly every day I dream up my hours and meetings with James Carlson Sweatt. I am a librarian, and you cannot stop me from annotating, revising, updating. I like to think that – because I am a librarian – I offer accurate and spurious advice with no judgment, good and bad next to each other on the shelf. But my memories are not books. Blessing if they were. Then maybe someone would borrow one and keep it too long and return it, a little battered, offering money for my forgiveness, each memory new after its long absence.

My memories are not books. They are only stories that I have been over so many times in my head that I don't know from one day to the next what's remembered and what's made up. Like when you memorize a poem, and for one small unimportant part you supply your own words. The meaning's the same, the meter's identical. When you read the actual version you can never get it into your head that it's right and you're wrong.

What I give you is the day's edition. Tomorrow it may be different.

I lived then, as now, in Brewsterville, an unremarkable little town on Cape Cod. Brewsterville lies halfway up the spit curl of the Cape, not close enough to the rest of the world to be convenient nor far enough to be attractively remote. We get tourists who don't know exactly what they've come out to see. Now we have little to show them: a few places that sell home-made jelly, a few guest houses, a small stretch of beach on the bay side. Our zoning laws keep us quaint, but just.

Once we had more. We had James Carlson Sweatt walking the streets. Some people came out specifically to visit James; some came for the ocean and happened upon him, more impressive than the ocean because no philosopher ever wonderingly addressed him, no poet compared him to God or a lover's restless body. Moreover, the ocean does not grant autographs. James did, politely, and then asked how you were enjoying your visit.

Everyone knew him as The Giant. Well, what else could you call him? Brilliant, maybe, and handsome and talented, but doomed to be mostly enormous. A painter, an amateur magician, a compulsive letter-writer, James Carlson Sweatt spent his life sitting down, hunching over. Hunching partly because that's the way he grew, like a flower; partly to make him seem smaller to others. Five feet tall in kindergarten; six foot two at age eleven. He turned sixteen and hit seven-five the same week.

The town's talking about building a statue to honor James, but there's a lot of bickering: for instance, what size? Life-sized puts it at about the same height as the statue of the town founder, who's life-and-a-half. Some people claim it'll attract tourists, who even now take pictures in front of the founder. Others maintain that tourists will take a picture of any old thing. 'Who's this behind me?' a lady tourist asks her husband, who is intent on his focusing.

'Pilgrims,' he answers.

For some people, history is simply what your wife looks good standing in front of. It's what's cast in bronze, or framed in sepia tones, or acted out with wax dummies and period furniture. It takes place in glass bubbles filled with water and chunks of plastic snow; it's stamped on souvenir pencils and summarized in reprint newspapers. History nowadays is recorded in memorabilia. If you can't purchase a shopping bag that alludes to something, people won't believe it ever happened.

Librarian (like Stewardess, Certified Public Accountant, Used Car Salesman) is one of those occupations that people assume attract a certain deformed personality. Librarians are supposed to be bitter spinsters; grudging, lonely. And above all stingy: we love our fine money, our silence.

I did not love fine money: I forgave much more than I collected. I did not shush people unless they yelled. And though I was technically a spinster, I was bitter only insofar as people made me. It isn't that bitter people become librarians; it's that being a librarian may turn the most giving person bitter. We are paid all day to be generous, and no one recognizes our generosity.

As a librarian, I longed to be acknowledged, even to be taken for granted. I sat at the desk, brimming with book reviews, information, warnings, all my good schooling, advice. I wanted people to constantly callously approach. But there were days nobody talked to me at all, they just walked to the shelves and grabbed a book and checked out, said, at most, *thank you*, and sometimes only *you're welcome* when I thanked them first. I had gone to school to learn how to help them, but they believed I was simply a clerk who stamped the books.

All it takes is a patron asking. And then asking again. A piece of paper covered with notes, the pencil smudged: a left-hander (for instance, James) will smudge more. The patron you become fond of will say, *I can't believe you have this book*. Or even better (believe it or not) *you don't own this book – is there a way I can get it?*

Yes.

Even at age eleven, twelve, James asked me how to find things in the catalog. He told me of books he liked, wanting something similar. He recognized me as an expert. Despite popular theories, I believe people fall in love based not on good looks or fate but on knowledge. Either they are amazed by something a beloved knows that they themselves do not know; or they discover common rare knowledge; or they can supply knowledge to someone who's lacking. Hasn't anyone found a strange ignorance in someone beguiling? An earnest question: what day of the week does Thanksgiving fall on this year? Nowadays, trendy librarians, wanting to be important, say, Knowledge is power. I know better. *Knowledge is love.*

People think librarians are unromantic, unimaginative. This is not true. We are people whose dreams run in particular ways. Ask a mountain climber what he feels when he sees a mountain; a lion tamer what goes through his mind when he meets a new lion; a doctor confronted with a beautiful malfunctioning body. The idea of a library full of books, the books full of knowledge, fills me with fear and love and courage and endless wonder. I knew I would be a librarian in college as a student assistant at a reference desk, watching those lovely people at work. 'I don't think there's such a book—' a patron would begin, and then the librarian would hand it to them, that very book.

Unromantic? This is a reference librarian's fantasy.

A patron arrives, says, Tell me something. You reach across the desk and pull him toward you, bear hug him a second and then take him into your lap, stroke his forehead, whisper facts in his ear. *The climate of Chad is tropical in the south, desert in the north. Source:* 1991 CIA World Factbook. *Do you love me? Americans consumed 6.2 gallons of tea per capita in 1989. Source:* Statistical Abstract of the United States. *Synecdoche is a literary device meaning the part for the whole, as in, the crowned heads of Europe. I love you. I could find you British Parliamentary papers, I could track down a book you only barely remember reading. Do you love me now? We own that book, we subscribe to that journal, Elvis Presley's first movie was called* Love Me Tender.

And then you lift the patron again, take him over the desk and set him down so gently he doesn't feel it, because there's someone else arriving, and she looks, oh, she looks *uninformed*.

He became a regular after that first school visit, took four books out at a time, returned them, took another four. I let him renew the magic book again and again, even though the rules said one renewal only. Librarians lose reason when it comes to the regulars, the good people, the *readers*. Especially when they're like James: it wasn't that he was lonely or bored; he wasn't dragged into the library by a parent. He didn't have that strange desperate look that some librarygoers develop, even children, the one that says: *this is the only place I'm welcome anymore.* Even when he didn't want advice, he'd approach the desk with notes crumpled up, warm from his palm, his palm gray from the graphite. He'd hold it out until I grabbed the wastebasket by its rim, swung it around and offered it; his paper would go thunking in.

James was an eccentric kid, my favorite kind. I never knew how much of this eccentricity was height. He sometimes seemed peculiarly young, since he had the altitude but not the attitude of a man; and yet there was something elderly about him, too. He never returned a book without telling me that it was on time. Every now and then, when he returned one late, he was nearly frantic, almost angry; I didn't know whether it was at me for requiring books back at a certain time, or with himself for disregarding the due date.

He'd been coming in for a year when I finally met his mother. I didn't know her by sight: she was an exotic thing, with blond wavy hair down her back like a teenager, though she was thirty-five, ten years older than me. Her full cotton skirt had some sort of gold-flecked frosting swirled over the print.

'My son needs books,' she said.

'Yes?' I did not like mothers who come in for their children; they are meddlesome. 'Where is he?'

'In the hospital, up to Boston,' she said. A doleful twang pinched her voice. 'He wants books on history.'

'How old is he?'

'Twelve-but-smart,' she said. She wouldn't look me in the eye, and she trilled her fingertips over the edge of the counter. 'Ummm . . . Robert the Bruce? Is that somebody?'

'Yes,' I said. James and I had been discussing him. 'Is this for James? Are you Mrs Sweatt?'

She bit her lip. I hadn't figured James for the offspring of a lip-biter. 'Do you know Jim?' she asked.

'Of course.'

'Of course,' she repeated, and sighed.

'He's here every week. He's in the hospital? Is there something wrong?'

'Is something wrong?' she said. 'Well, nothing new. He's gone to an endocrinologist.' She pronounced each syllable of this last word like a word itself. 'Maybe they'll operate.'

'For what?' I asked.

'For *what?*' she said. 'For *him*. To slow him down.' She waved her hand above her head, to indicate excessive height. 'They're *alarmed*.'

'Oh. I'm sorry.'

'It's not good for him. I mean, it wouldn't be good for anyone to grow like that.'

'No, of course not.'

He must have known that he was scheduled to go to the hospital, and I was hurt he hadn't mentioned it.

'I was thinking Mark Twain too,' she said. 'For him to read. *Tom Sawyer* or something.'

'Fiction,' I said. 'Third floor. Clemens.'

'Clemens,' she repeated. She loved the taste of other people's words in her mouth.

'*Clemens*,' I said. 'Mark Twain, Samuel Clemens. That's where we file him.'

Before his mother had come to the library, I hadn't

73

realized that there was anything medically wrong with James. He was tall, certainly, but in the same sweet gawky way young men are often tall. His bones had great plans, and the rest of him, voice and skin balance, strained to keep pace. He bumped into things and walked on the sides of his feet and his hair would not stay in a single configuration for more than fifteen minutes. He was not even a teenager yet; he had not outgrown childhood freckles or enthusiasms.

They didn't operate on James that hospital visit. The diagnoses: tall, very. Chronic, congenital height. He came back with more wrong than he left with: an orderly, pushing him down the hall, misguessed a corner and cracked his ankle.

He was twelve years old then, and six foot four.

The Assumption of Mrs Sweatt

I sometimes got into disagreements with patrons. They were rare. Despite my clumsiness with the outside world, I was the perfect public servant: deferential, dogged, oblivious to insults. Friendly but not overly familiar. It was one of the reasons I loved being a librarian: I got to conduct dozens of relationships simultaneously and successfully. I conformed myself always to the needs of the patrons (they certainly did not care about mine), told them they were right, called them Mr and Mrs and Miss when they did not bother to learn my smallest initial. Do you wonder why we're called public *servants*?

Every now and then, though, I would have a run-in with a patron who demanded something preposterous. Maybe they wanted me to immediately hand over a book so popular that others had been waiting months for it; maybe they wanted to supply a page-long shopping list of books so I could pull them off the shelves. Maybe they wanted not to be charged a penny for their enormous fines because they had been too busy to get to the library. (The most unmanageable patrons always told me how *busy* they were.) I'd say, politely, no. They'd say yes. I got firm; they got insulting. I'd start to explain my position in depth, they'd ask to see a manager – and then I'd bow my head (I *loved* this moment) and say, 'I am Miss Cort, the director of the library.' It was not a title I ever otherwise claimed.

I longed to say, Listen: in my library, as in the Kingdom of Heaven, the rude and busy are not rewarded. We honor manners, patience, good deeds, and grave misfortune only.

And one of two things happened: the patrons returned, and either thought I'd forgotten what had happened or had forgotten themselves, and were amazed when I politely, smilingly remembered them by name.

Or they never came back.

James and I had not argued, but I'd felt I'd done something much worse in so misunderstanding what he'd wanted, in giving him *Medical Curiosities*. I could forgive myself social clumsiness, my occasional crippling shyness, a sharp tongue at the wrong time. I could not forgive sloppy library work, and that is what I was guilty of: a patron – my best, most beloved patron – needed help in finding something, and I'd jumped to a conclusion and given him books that were worse than useless. He'd asked me a straightforward question and I had not come close to providing an answer.

But he returned the next Friday, with a different question. I still remember: he wanted to know what an anti-Pope was.

Maybe it was forgiveness, and maybe it was just teenage obliviousness, but the sight of James that afternoon seemed miraculous. *You came back*, I said to him as I sent him to the card catalog ('Look under Catholic Church – history') and he said, *Sure, Peggy, where else would I go?*

I watched him read that afternoon. He sat at the table in the front room – his favored spot, ever since his first visit. Looking over his shoulders, I could see his book through the edge of his glasses. The words slid in curves as he moved his head.

I wanted to stand there forever, see what he saw. Not

possible, of course. He'd stand up and take those glasses with him. I could only see through them now, me standing and him sitting, hunched significantly over, because he needed a stronger prescription. His eyes were growing at a different rate from the rest of him and would not stay in focus.

Caroline had an easy pregnancy. I'd expected that she would. It was as if the new stomach that swelled in front of her were something she'd expected all her life, an addition that she'd been meaning for years to install. Some women move into their bellies when they're pregnant; it's everything they think of, it's what they move first and most carefully. Not Caroline. She lived in her whole easy body, barely changed her flat-footed gait.

I myself hardly noticed my physical self, which I considered a not-too-useful appendage. Only my feet demanded my attention. When I wore a bad pair of shoes on a busy day, my fet swelled, complained. I was forced to think of them, to picture getting home and slipping off my shoes, the way a starving man will torture and comfort himself with fantasies of food. Nothing to do – I could not pad around the library stocking-footed. My mouth answered questions, but I was stuck in my throbbing feet.

My feet were wide, wide, wide, and flat-footed, which was mostly a blessing – no arches to ache or fall. Nevertheless, by the time I was in my mid-twenties, they were an old person's feet, bunioned and calloused and noisome and shapeless and yellowed. Blue veins ran the length; my toes, forced into tiny places for years, huddled together for comfort. I didn't mind so much: it was as if I knew what I would look like as a senior citizen, from the ground up.

James caught me late on Friday at the library, a week after his return. (Though he hadn't actually been gone, I always thought of it that way, *his return*.) I'd taken off a shoe and put it on the counter, searching for the boulder I felt sure was somewhere around the toe. Probably it was just a piece of sand. This close to the ocean, you always have sand in your shoes, embedded in your carpet, even if you never go to the beach.

'Your shoes bother you?' he asked.

'Oh,' I said. I shook out the shoe, dropped it to the floor, and stepped into it. I walked around to the front of the desk, trying to get the shoe jammed on; on top of everything, it was a little too small. 'Always, I'm afraid. Usually. That's what happens when you're on your feet all day.'

'What size do you wear?' he asked.

'Five and a half,' I said, automatically shaving a full size off. 'Women's. Different from men's.'

'I know. I wear a man's thirty,' he said. Then he saw the surprise on my face and laughed. 'Five times bigger. More than five times.' He stood beside me and steadied himself with his hand on my head. I didn't take it personally – he often steadied himself with the closest person; it was usually the handiest thing. Then he took his hand away.

'Look,' he said. He'd lined up his foot with mine. They didn't even look like the same part of the body, his high black shoe next to my white pump.

'Your feet are wide,' he said.

'Yes.'

'So you wear a five and a half wide?'

'Five and a half, six wide.'

'Which one?'

'Okay,' I said. 'You caught me in a vain lie. Six wide. Honest.'

'Vanity is saying you wear smaller shoes than you really do?'

'Well,' I said. I blushed. 'For some of us, it is. Women, I mean.'

Two weeks later he brought me a small cardboard box.

'I got these for you,' he said.

Inside were a pair of sensible oxblood lace-ups. Old-lady shoes. The good tangy smell of leather floated up.

'James,' I said. 'You bought me shoes.' I could not

remember the last time someone had given me a gift, other than the occasional Christmas box of chocolates from a patron.

'Well, I got them,' he said. 'These are good for your feet. I just started working for a shoe store. They make all my shoes.'

I tried to picture James sitting on a shoe saleman's slanty stool. He would not fit.

'You're selling shoes?' I asked.

'Sort of.' He lifted one of the shoes out of the box and held it in his hand. 'I'm going to do personal appearances. you know, show up. Look tall. And they'll make my shoes for free.'

'No pay?'

'Shoes are expensive,' he said. 'My shoes are, anyhow.' He looked back down at his feet. 'Maybe I'll go to New York.'

'This shoe store is in New York?'

He shook his head. 'Hyannis. But there's an expo in New York in the spring.' He pointed with the shoe in his hand at the shoes on my feet, navy blue snub-nosed pumps. 'You shouldn't wear those,' he said. 'They're bad for your feet. These' – he handed me the shoe – 'they have ankle support and arch support and everything. I talked to the shoe guy. I was just going to get you black, and he wanted to talk me into pink. I knew you wouldn't wear pink shoes.'

'I wouldn't,' I said. 'That's true.'

'So we compromised on red. Reddish brown, anyhow.'

'They're wonderful,' I said.

'Try them on. Might be a little stiff at first, but they'll wear in. The shoe guys break mine in for me with a machine, but they know exactly how my toes go. They've got a cast of my foot. A couple of casts. They've got one they're going to put in the window, and a shoe in my size that they're going to bronze and hang outside. I have to sit down now,' he told me. 'Try them on.'

He went to one of the library's older chairs – the nineteenth-century furniture fit him best; the newer stuff was blocky and ungenerous – and dragged it close so he could watch me.

I knew, looking at the shoes, that they would be murder. True, they had ankle support. And arch support, but for someone as flat-footed as I was – and getting more flat-footed every year – that would hurt, not help. Most important was the missing half-size I had shaved off, out of vanity's sake. Now what difference would a half-size smaller foot have made to a sixteen-year-old boy, especially one who wore size thirty shoes?

They'd put a little broguing around the toes of the shoes – to make them feminine, no doubt. They reminded me of the sort of boots sullen young girls of the gay nineties wore. I picked one up.

Luckily, I could get my foot in. I was glad James had made me confess to the additional half-size. I bent down to lace it up, disappearing behind the circulation desk. The shoe had a bracing, athletic feel.

'Try them both,' he said, straining to see me over the desk. 'I can take them back for adjustments. Get them to stretch out parts.'

I'd deliberately chosen the left shoe, since my left foot was slightly smaller than my right. But I put the other on, laced it up.

'Walk in them,' James said. 'Make sure they fit.' He sounded like my mother, school-clothes shopping.

I took a few steps. It seemed like a miracle, and I the heroine of a fairy tale. They fit. They were rigid and, truth be told, unflattering, but what did I have that needed so badly to be flattered? I walked around the front of the desk and wriggled my toes for him.

'Okay?' he said.

'I love them.'

'But do they *fit?*' asked James, ever practical.

'Of course,' I said. 'I couldn't love anything that didn't fit.'

'Aunt Caroline says I shouldn't take advantage of the shoe store, but they told me I could have as many pairs of shoes as I want, just ask. I was going to get a pair for Mom, but I didn't.'

I'd been admiring the shiny uncreased toes of my shoes. When I looked up at James, he was staring at my feet.

'Why not?'

'She only wears tennis shoes now, when she wears them at all. Mostly she just sleeps or stays on the sofa.'

At first I wasn't sure I wanted to talk about Mrs Sweatt. 'How's she feeling these days?'

'Um. The same, I think. Aunt Caroline thinks better, but I don't. She doesn't get out much. You should come see her.'

'Oh,' I said.

'Oh, well. I don't blame you for not wanting to.'

'It's not that. It's just – well, maybe when she feels better.'

'Sure,' said James. He smiled at me. 'Whenever that is.'

Though I loved my shoes (they are even now in their original box, worn once, immaculate), I did not love the fact of the shoe store. How was this different, I wondered, from Anna Swann in Barnum's museum? In those days I still imagined James could have a career other than Acting Tall, that being inspected by the curious was fine on a volunteer basis (in the summer he could not help it) but was not a sensible profession.

'So,' I said to Caroline when she came to see me the next Monday. 'James has a job.'

'He does?' she said. She took her spot at the front table; it was quiet, so I went to join her. 'How wonderful.'

'You don't know about the shoe store?'

'Oh, *that*,' she said. 'I never really thought of that as a job. He's just going to be there twice a year, walk around.'

'And perhaps go to New York for them?'

'Yes,' she said. 'He's looking forward to that.'

'A lot of responsibility for a boy.'

'Good for him,' said Caroline. 'And that way the shoes are free.'

'When I was a girl,' I said, 'I didn't have to work for my shoes – '

Caroline took my hand across the library table. 'When you were a girl,' she said quietly, 'you didn't wear size thirty shoes. Peggy, if I could buy them for him, I would. But being that tall is an expensive proposition. I can't tell you. It's not like we're rich people. I mean, we do our best, but shoes cost seventy-five dollars, and clothing as much or more. Mrs Sweatt can't do a thing for him. I mean, she does plenty *for* him, they talk, she loves him – well, that's neither here nor there. If I could go to the shoe store, walk around for him, I would, I promise you.' She laughed, laid one hand on her stomach. 'Goodness knows I feel like the biggest woman in the world, but they're not offering free shoes to *me*.'

At home that night, I looked at my shoes and thought of Mrs Sweatt, napping on her sofa in her sneakers. All I had wanted was to become part of that family. And not even an important part: a trusted maid, perhaps, a cousin several times removed. But Mrs Sweatt stamped her foot, told her sister-in-law never to invite me back. I loved seeing Caroline and James at my library, but I was still being simply a librarian.

I was a fool. Foolish to imagine making myself part of a family that was not mine; foolish to think that people thought of me as anything but the librarian, a plain, no-nonsense, uninteresting person. Foolish to imagine myself some Hans Christian Andersen princess in those damn shoes, possessor of the only feet to inhabit the magic oxfords, especially since by the end of that day my feet – as if they might really have been momentarily bewitched into submission by the shoes – assumed their true size, and cursed at me bitterly for shutting them up in those leather dungeons.

81

AAMER HUSSEIN

Dreaming of Java

Loneliness, fleeing from your body like the smell of poverty, playing light-games on your skin, invisible: you sense it, I can tell, but refuse to see it.

That first time, when I noticed you: you walked down the stairs and saw me. You seemed to follow me to the spot where I sat. I only saw you later. I looked up from my book, inadvertently, and your eyes saw mine: you smiled.

That first encounter, of words that don't matter, of gestures that never found their tongue. But you tied me to you: in that hold I cannot, will not break.

A man from China. Five years before I'd read a book in which a Chinaman initiates a child into a world of love. But I was not a child – and you were not that man.

Ah, that loneliness, transcending language, flowing from your skin like the smell of love. It bound me to you, an answer to that ancient tongue of gestures frozen in my barren lands. Man from China. Born when I was two, you grew up without a childhood. Hungry in the years of the great famine, moving from aunt to uncle to aunt in the years of the Cultural Revolution when your renegade parents were sent away for re-education, working away your adolescent years in a bath-house, spared the coun-tryside indignities of your contemporaries. At twenty you went to university to study physics: you taught science for five years in the city of your birth. Man from Beijing. You left your city short weeks after the events of Tiananmen; you abandoned your physics to study philosophy in this strange country. Lived in a series of attics and cellars, survived on white bread and jam and boiled butterfly pasta. When you return to China – if you return – you may never share what you learnt in your months of aching foreignness with following generations. Then again, as changes sweep your country as I yearn for them to come to mine, perhaps you will.

Tiananmen. Shadows of young bodies, images in black and white, fall on our first meetings. Nine months after the happening. Are the furrows of your face, glimpsed in unguarded moments, guardians of silent testimony, of secrets you'll never reveal? Does the dullness of your shoulders, glimpsed in unguarded moments, bear quiet witness to grief? But I won't ask you painful questions. I'll speak instead of troubled times, and of the madness of these times, a madness only for the sane to understand, to regain their sanity. I'll chant to you my litany of names: Karachi, Jaisalmer, Java, Bombay, Benazir, Rongowarsito, Bangladesh, Beijing. You still live in the Third World, you can say, but the third world is a state of mind. Have you seen the Wayang Purwa? I will ask. If in the theatre of shadows you sit behind the screen, you can see the puppets' black and golden forms, you can see the Dalang and the orchestra. But you and I, ordinary spectators, trapped in our emotions' shadow-theatre, watch forms elusive, veiled. And if we tear the screen away? Not yet, not yet.

Tonight I will speak to you of Java. Look: my hands are black and golden puppets, my body is a Dalang. In ten short days I will fly on the back of a golden bird to sleep in the bed of a dark poet who loves me. In her skin I'll seek refuge from my centuries of landlessness and longing for a home, in her words I'll look for the answers that your lips will never utter. I will speak to you of a country that like my mind has known devastation, whose people like my tongue have been colonized. Of a terrain uncharted by my pen, lying like the map of my body bathed in a sun that doesn't warm you, but continues to burn me and the islands in a threnody of dreams you long to master, islands yet unknown to you and me of which I sing to snare you in my net of words.

But you, too, can wrap me in your shadows: of sorrow. Ah, those furrows on your face: you too have been abandoned. Days before you left Beijing you were divorced, by a woman whose love gave you seven months of solace before you ran, from what you describe in your stuttering grief as her greed. Yes, she left you for another man, I know, I understand, I've been there and returned, your body feels so heavy when somebody's gone, you drag your feet and bear your weight, easier to wrap your arms around yourself if you can lie yourself to sleep, they don't last, these stories, you ride them for a year or two then don't know whose corpse is heavier, yours or mine, it's a burning sea or a deep blue story told in a foreign language, your body is the gap between yourself and her when someone leaves, leaves the story you didn't know how to write, you keep writing in the third person about tormented men, they always like the third person past tense, the text keeps changing form. As the night deepens with the furrows of your face I will listen. As the shadows of your pain flicker on the night's white screen I will listen. If you ask for the story of my life I'll tell you my past doesn't have a face, that the 'I' by which I call myself doesn't exist, only throws a shadow. If you ask for the meaning of the word 'love' I'll tell you I don't know, it's strange to me, a void, like writing, or an absence, like God. So I'll tell you of the sunsets of my mind which I stole from my city by the sea, hibiscus-red like the blood in which I dip my words, gold-rimmed roses embroidered on black like the dreams of Java that warm my April nights, which I'll leave with you to lift you from your sorrow. Because you haven't known the emptiness of writing and God. So tonight, I will leave you.

If you ask me to tell you of a woman who is slowly fading, the one who took me on a carpet of camellias when I was twenty-five and she was twice my age, who said she'd cage me or let me fly as long as she could keep me, the one with needle tracks along her wasting arms and legs, who said I was the monsoon rain of Chittagong because she couldn't keep me out though she barred her windows, the one who lied to me when she said she'd marry me, who sent me back to recover branches broken by my father from the frangipani and the almond in my mother's garden, for whom I found the dying forts of Jaisalmer and came back dreaming I was dead and dragged by horses through the white dunes of God's abandoned desert, for whom I wrote my false name on the sand because I thought the white sheets were the deserts of Thar and Rohi and her name was written on the walls that were the sky and they told me I was mad, the one I called a hibiscus – (Allah, Allah, they used to sing, those passing minstrels of my childhood, a string breaks and no one hears, I heard them when I closed my eyes to die again of being me) – no, if you ask me of these things I will not speak because if I do you'll ask me to stay the night and I can't. It's not your fault. My stories won't console you. Dreams, passion, death, sex, God, my words are only shadows on a screen. It doesn't matter. I haven't learnt a thing.

So I leave you with the rancid and unfinished wine you won't dare to drink alone, with that stammering story of your broken marriage, with your smell of loneliness that scares me because it asks me to touch you and my hands are strapped to these hammers that want to strike the haunted chords of the gamelan, keen the songs of Java. I won't touch you because the keys of your bones compose minor chords I can't understand. Your desire for me doesn't have a skin, it's all glass, fragile and sharp enough to cut these hands that yearn to be healed again to write of Java.

Strangled laments, dead loves, estrangement from my
native lands, forbidden pacts and words condemned to
constraints of secret messages, you will never learn to ask
me of these things and I won't ever learn to touch you with
my frozen fingers. Allah, Allah, a string . . . my hands, if
you could see my hands, the shadows of my hands . . .

> listen, someone in pain is passing by. I can hear her
> bracelets crying
> against clouds of charcoal smoke a scattering flock of
> pink pigeons says: the night's nearly done
> soft, light, I fall, I flow. I am a lamp on waves. Or a boat of
> poppies floating into absence.

Now I'm back from Java; trapped again in wastelands of white
paper. You're angry with my shadow, I know I've been inept:
I've stepped on something you guard from me. I haven't
spoken of the gnawing hole inside, wrapping you instead in
the noisy light of my success in Jakarta – drinking with poets
and singers and breaking my promise to my poet who lies
awake beside my ungiving body. I've seen villages and canals
and palaces and painted dancers but failed to reach my
dream-temples of Borobudur and Prambanan – I've only
stroked their shadows. The gods' leather bodies lie dead in
bright trappings, buried in puppet-masters' wooden chests:
but Javanese remember the colours of divine desires concealed
behind white screens. Mine was a fleeting victory; as you said,
we poets and writers leave no trace, our words mere shadows
on a screen. The echoes of our quiet voices die with our lovers,
or with the corpses of our loves that fail to live.

I'm back, with wings alight. Like ardent Wayang heroes
I've mistaken a beloved's beauty for God's face: illusion or
reality, what difference does it make, if you can count the
colours? But you couldn't fathom the colours of a new pact:
I'd thought it was a pond, pellucid, clear enough for you to
see the blue and red and yellow fish within. But only stones
for you. So I'm waiting, for leave to drain the lake; written
into a place of powerlessness by your decree. Who's the

puppeteer? you asked me one day and I should have known how to say, not I, not I; we're both driven by something we can't combat. But it seemed easier then to see you as the impassive fickle Dalang and me, a hapless shadow.

Speak to me, I call out to you from the white screen waste. I'm a child of the Sindh, born between the desert and the sea. In the city of my birth the sun set in the sea and the sky drowned in a crazy net of colours. My mother threw stones at the coconut tree and all of us would drink the nectar from the nut. We lived on a hill. It didn't rain in the desert but when it did we'd run out, naked, let the downpour drench our skins. The earth smelt of longing and falling jasmine flowers. A peacock flew into our garden and stayed four days. Its owner came and took it away. I was seven. I think that was the last time I cried.

Then my father cut the branches of my mother's trees and left her bangles crying. I don't remember if that was before the war and the great locust plague. The garden was ravaged and we ran out of food. We learnt to look for roots and drink the syrup from the stalks of certain flowers. But she'd go out looking, looking for food; eat, she'd say, the children must eat. And one day they came and took her away for months. We were left alone. She came back frozen, she thought the soldiers had come to get us or that they were cutting the country up again. They were. A new land was born that they called Bangladesh but we crossed another border into my mother's country. Allah, Allah, we said, you break our strings and no one hears. But there in the Blue Mountains where hyenas howled and the wind blew black I learnt to love a boy who took me on a golden bird's back to Java in his dreams. My first friend. The name by which they called him sounded like the last syllable of God's name. Once in the school yard I shouted out for him so loud they came to cut my tongue off at the root. I was fourteen. That must have been the last time I called out someone's name. And you didn't answer.

*

87

I've been silent, ever since. But then perhaps my voiceless anguish touched you. Or the memory of my Javan dreams. Once again you searched for me: in Toilet Paper Town, where people slept in cardboard boxes, in quiet or in crowded places, between rows of books perishing on dusty shelves, by railway station stalls or in halls where, desultory, the shadows of my hands played pictures of a crazy moth on fire, you'd find me at my games.

Look, I said: I never loved you and I never would. Written into my corner, my place of powerlessness, I said: I can never touch you. I can't even imagine you naked. Your body speaks a strange language that I can't understand. I can't fathom the gestures of your hands. You're a mystery, like writing, or an absence, like God.

But we can speak of Java, you said. (Though you'd changed your focus to Balinese cockfights.) Talk to me of the Wayang Purwa or Rongowarsito. That's what you Indus people have in common with the Javanese: you share heresies.

Yes, I responded, they have their Dalang and we our mystic bards. No temples, we say, except those of the heart. Whores are better than princesses because they dance to please their lovers and dogs more faithful than priests because they know more about unconditional love.

And we would speak again of troubled times, of China and Benazir. I'd been back to Karachi, where they were chasing people into the sea. But the sea, too, had been chased away from its shores. They've taken away my waves, my brothers at war. Leave, leave, my friends had said: the sky doesn't need you, the sea is saying goodbye. In my mother's India the armies of the Left and the Right were amassing for battle. Television screens, shadow-theatres of today, showed preparations for the new production of the Mahabharata. Muslim or Hindu, sibling against sibling, cousins at war, arraying themselves in ritual gestures, arming themselves with archaic weapons. But who are the Kauravas and who the Pandavas? A confusion of roles, I said. Alarmed by this chronicle of fratricide, the Dalang has lost the script, forgotten the answers.

All my countries – motherland, fatherland – on fire. I'd gambled: been outbid on every piece of ground on which I'd hoped to build a shack. Except Java. I had set aside my books of Farid, Abdul Latif and Bulle Shah; I was looking for that quietness of which Rongowarsito writes, surpassing heresy and passion. And while I tried to be a brother to trees and stones, I'd drink wine with you, ask about your lovers or the whiteness of your nights. Or speak of Beijing. Benazir fell again. Leaves were thick golden pulp on rain-sodden pavements. Autumn, you said, is short in Beijing, but beautiful. The kind of season we could live in for ever. One autumn you should visit Beijing. And write about it. And one day you can take me to the temples of Java.

But then the dark moon would swallow you again, chew you up and spit you out; you would speak of death and the loneliness of all living. Or you'd long again for China. I'm going home, what's the use of all this? I'm going to be a farmer on the land. When you come to see me I'll slaughter a whole pig . . . ah, but you don't eat pork . . .

Or you'd look around you here and see decay and dereliction, speak of some drunken youth with pierced lip and shaven skull who'd crushed a bottle in his hands, slashing his palms to drink, in rapture, his own blood. First World, Third World, it's all the same, you said, but you with your belief in fate and puppeteers, you only look at dreams. It's all a matter of chance; accidents and collisions . . . Fate, accidents, collisions, what's the difference? I interrupted. All in the hands of a Dalang without a script, improvising a random entertainment. Because in my state of hallucinated tranquillity I still felt the reflected stirrings of some madness, yours, perhaps. Ours was a bond of silence. We were companions in a twisted night of absence. I'd jokingly call us a two-man community of pain. So in those half-lit autumn afternoons I learnt to move away from you, to recognize the contours of your bones beneath the furrows, to interpret the real lines of your face's cheating text with its assembly of meanings. And then your startling winter smile: for that I would have paid a thousand Java summers.

I thought then of the winter: how instead of Java I would find, here in this leaden city, safe in a world of masks and shadows, the companion who would drink with me these stories of rupture and discontinuity, and how in turn I'd learn a dialect of love without clauses of ownership, belonging or claim.

Too late, though. Java staked its claim on me again. Temples had been waiting too long: the tall stones and the stupas, the palm trees and the figurines placed on sacred branches in courtyards by ponds full of blue and red and yellow fish – stolen centuries ago, or a gift from some ancient emperor of China, perhaps.

And for you, a wedding. No temples. For on a Thursday afternoon – as the October sun suddenly appeared to take the weary longing from my skull and replace it with contentment – (behind you, a grey woman digging in a dustbin for cake crumbs to soak up her supper of gin) – you told me of the woman you'd marry. Too long, you said, without a resting place: I need a home. I'd seen you with her many times (once in Trafalgar Square). The picture I'll carry in the album of my memories until it's mislaid: the two of you, standing together like the sentinel deities of one of my temples, at the portals of some profane and splendid shrine. This is how I'll remember you, man from Beijing, bitter stories of unloving now behind you, terrified of a poet's damned life of shadows, ready once again to take your secular vows.

Next month, you said, I want to be married. (Your declaration's sharp delicate delineations as formal as Chinese calligraphy.) I would like you to be there at my wedding dinner. And though I'll understand if you refuse, I would also like you to witness the registration of my marriage.

You may have miscalculated my response as you sat under a stunted tree with sunlight's final breath turning your cheekbones to dusk. (Behind you, the grey woman finishing her supper of pastry crumbs.) Because as I reached out to cover your hand with mine the smell of loneliness engulfed me once again, flowing from your skin like a cry.

I am calm.

Felicitations, I say. But by then I'll be dreaming of Java. I will buy a puppet from the puppet maker and place it with a vow and a prayer for your happiness in a niche between two branches of a banana tree. I'll search for blue and red and yellow fish in a palace courtyard in Surakarta. Are those fish from China? Can you tell me? I'll stand on the seashore shedding beads of hibiscus blood for the head-snakes of Ratu Kidul. I'll bathe in the fires of the sun, let it tan and flay my skin for the drum of a passing musician, bleach my bones for its flute. I'll dance in the glory of Yang Maha Kuasa. I'll wake in the arms of a poet, sleep by the grave of a saint, dream beneath the carved breasts of goddesses on the floor of Prambanan, and rest in the stone hand of God.

SIR ROBERT AYTOUN

'Upone Tabacco'

Forsaken of all comforts but these two,
My faggott and my Pipe, I sitt and Muse
On all my crosses, and almost accuse
The heavens for dealing with me as they do.
Then hope steps in and with a smyling brow
Such chearfull expectations doth infuse
As makes me think ere long I cannot chuse
But be some Grandie, whatsoever I'm now.
But having spent my pipe, I then perceive
That hopes and dreams are Couzens, both deceive.
Then make I this conclusion in my mind,
Its all one thing, both tends unto one Scope
To live upon Tabacco and on hope,
The one's but smoake, the other is but wind.

VLADIMIR NABOKOV

In Memory of L. I. Shigaev

Leonid Ivanovich Shigaev is dead . . . The suspension dots, customary in Russian obituaries, must represent the footprints of words that have departed on tiptoe, in reverent single file, leaving their tracks on the marble . . . However, I would like to violate this sepulchral silence. Please allow me to . . . Just a few fragmentary, chaotic, basically uncalled-for . . . But no matter. He and I met about eleven years ago, in a year that for me was disastrous. I was virtually perishing. Picture to yourself a young, still very young, helpless and lonely person, with a perpetually inflamed soul (it feared the least contact, it was like raw flesh) and unable to cope with the pangs of an unhappy love affair . . . I shall take the liberty of dwelling on this point for a moment.

There was nothing exceptional about that thin, bobhaired German girl, but when I used to look at her, at her suntanned cheek, at her rich fair hair, whose shiny, golden-yellow and olive-gold strands sloped so roundly in profile from crown to nape, I felt like howling with tenderness, a tenderness that just would not fit inside me simply and comfortably, but remained wedged in the door and would not bulge in or out – bulky, brittle-cornered and of no use to anyone, least of all to that lass. In short, I discovered that once a week, at her house, she betrayed me with a respectable paterfamilias, who, incidentally, was so infernally meticulous that he would bring his own shoe trees with him. It all ended with the circuslike whump of a monstrous box on the ear with which I knocked down the traitress, who rolled up in a ball where she had collapsed, her eyes glistening at me through her spread fingers – all in all quite flattered, I think. Automatically, I searched for something to throw at her, saw the china sugar bowl I had given her for Easter, took the thing under my arm and went out, slamming the door.

A footnote: this is but one of the conceivable versions of my parting with her; I had considered many of these impossible possibilities while still in the first heat of my drunken delirium, imagining now the gross gratification of a good slap; now the firing of an old Parabellum pistol, at her and at myself, at her and at the paterfamilias, only at her, only at myself; then, finally, a glacial irony, noble sadness, silence – oh, things can go in so many ways, and I have long since forgotten how they actually went.

My landlord at the time, an athletic Berliner, suffered permanently from furunculosis: the back of his neck showed a square of disgustingly pink sticking paster with three neat apertures – for ventilation, maybe, or for the release of the pus. I worked in an émigré publishing house for a couple of languid-looking individuals who in reality were such cunning crooks that plain people upon observing them got spasms in the chest, as when one steps onto a cloud-piercing summit. As I began coming late ('systematically late' as they called it) and missing work, or arriving in such condition that it was necessary to send me home, our relationship became unbearable, and finally, thanks to a joint effort – with the enthusiastic collaboration of the bookkeeper and of some stranger who had come in with a manuscript – I was thrown out.

My poor, my pitiful youth! I vividly visualize the ghastly little room that I rented for five dollars a month, the ghastly flowerets of the wallpaper, the ghastly lamp hanging from its cord, with a naked bulb whose manic light glowed sometimes till morn. I was so miserable there, so indecently, luxuriously miserable, that the walls to this day must be saturated with misfortune and fever, and it is unthinkable that some happy chap could have lived there after me, whistling, humming. Ten years have elapsed, and even now I can still imagine myself then, a pale youth seated in front of the shimmery mirror, with his livid forehead and black beard, dressed only in a torn shirt, guzzling cheap booze and clinking glasses with his reflection. What times those were! Not only was I of no use to anyone in the world, but I could not even imagine a set of circumstances in which someone might care a whit about me.

By dint of prolonged, persistent, solitary drinking I drove myself to the most vulgar of visions, the most Russian of all hallucinations: I began seeing devils. I saw them every evening as soon as I emerged from my diurnal dreamery to dispel with my wretched lamp the twilight that was already engulfing us. Yes, even more clearly than I now see the perpetual tremor of my hand, I saw the precious intruders and after some time I even became accustomed to their presence, as they kept pretty much to themselves. They were smallish but rather plump, the size of an overweight toad – peaceful, limp, black-skinned, more or less warty little monsters. They crawled rather than walked, but, with all their feigned clumsiness, they proved uncapturable. I remember buying a dog whip and, as soon as enough of them had gathered on my desk, I tried to give them a good lashing, but they miraculously avoided the blow; I struck again, and one of them, the nearest, only blinked, screwing up his eyes crookedly, like a tense dog that someone wishes to threaten away from some tempting bit of ordure. The others dispersed, dragging their hind legs. But they all stealthily clustered together again while I wiped up the ink spilled on the desk and picked up a prostrate portrait. Generally speaking, their densest habitat was the vicinity of my writing table; they materialized from somewhere underneath and, in leisurely fashion, their sticky bellies crepitating and smacking against the wood, made their way up the desk legs, in a parody of climbing sailors. I tried smearing their route with Vaseline but this did not help, and only when I happened to select some particularly appetizing little rotter, intently clambering upward, and swatted him with the whip or with my shoe, only then did he fall on the floor with a fat-toad thud; but a minute later there he was again, on his way up from a different corner, his violet tongue hanging out from the strain, and once over the top he would join his comrades. They were numerous, and at first they all seemed alike to me: dark little creatures with puffy, basically rather good-natured faces; they sat in groups of five or six on the desk, on various papers, on a volume of Pushkin, glancing at me with indifference. One of them might scratch behind his ear with his foot, the long claw making a coarse scraping sound, and then freeze motionless, forgetting his leg in midair. Another would doze, uncomfortably crowding his neighbor, who, for that matter, was not blameless either: the reciprocal inconsiderateness of amphibians, capable of growing torpid in intricate attitudes. Gradually I began distinguishing them, and I think I even gave them names depending on their resemblance to acquaintances of mine or to various animals. One could make out larger and smaller specimens (although they were all of quite portable size), some were more repulsive, others more acceptable in aspect, some had lumps or tumors, others were perfectly smooth. A few had a habit of spitting at each other. Once they brought a new boy, an albino, of a cinereous tint, with eyes like beads of red caviar; he was very sleepy and glum, and gradually crawled away. With an effort of will I would manage to vanquish the spell for a moment. It was an agonizing effort, for I had to repel and hold away a horrible iron weight, for which my entire being served as a magnet: I had but to loosen my grip, to give in ever so slightly, and the phantasma would take shape again, becoming precise, growing stereoscopic, and I would experience a deceptive sense of relief – the relief of despair, alas – when I once again yielded to the hallucination, and once again the clammy mass of thick-skinned clods sat before me on the desk, looking at me sleepily and yet somehow expectantly. I tried not only the whip, but also a famous time-honored method, on which I now find myself embarrassed to enlarge, especially since I must have used it in some wrong, very wrong way. Still, the first time it did work: a certain sacramental sign with bunched fingers, pertaining to a particular religious cult, was unhurriedly performed by me at a height of a few inches above the compact group of devils and grazed them like a red-hot iron, with a succulent hiss, both pleasant and nasty; whereupon, squirming from their burns, my rascals disparted and dropped with ripe plops to the floor. But, when I repeated the experiment with a new gathering, the effect proved weaker and after that they stopped reacting altogether, that is, they very quickly developed a certain immunity . . . but enough about that. With a laugh – what else did I have left? – I would utter 'T'foo!' (the only expletive, by the way, borrowed by the Russian language from the lexicon of devils; see also the German 'Teufel'), and, without undressing, go to bed (on top of the covers, of course, as I was afraid of encountering unwanted bedfellows). Thus the days passed, if one can call them days – these were not days, but a timeless fog – and when I came to I found myself rolling on the floor, grappling with my hefty landlord among the shambles of the furniture. With a desperate lunge I freed myself and flew out of the room and thence on to the stairs, and the next thing I knew I was walking down the street, trembling, disheveled, a vile bit of alien plaster sticking to my fingers, with an aching body and a ringing head, but almost totally sober.

That was when L. I. took me under his wing. 'What's the matter, old man?' (We already knew each other slightly; he had been compiling a Russian–German pocket dictionary of technical terms and used to visit the office where I worked.) 'Wait a minute, old man, just look at yourself.' Right there on the corner (he was coming out of a delicatessen shop with his supper in his briefcase) I burst into tears, and, without a word, L. I. took me to his place, installed me on the sofa, fed me liverwurst and beef-tea, and spread over me a quilted overcoat with a worn astrakhan collar. I shivered and sobbed, and presently fell asleep.

In short, I remained in his little apartment, and lived like that for a couple of weeks, after which I rented a room next door, and we continued seeing each other daily. And yet, who would think we had anything in common? We were different in every respect! He was nearly twice my age, dependable, debonair, portly, dressed generally in a cutaway coat, cleanly and thriftily, like the majority of our orderly, elderly émigré bachelors: it was worth seeing, and especially hearing, how methodically he brushed his trousers in the morning: the sound of that brushing is now so intimately associated with him, so prominent in my recollection of him – especially the rhythm of the process, the pauses between spells of scraping, when he would stop to examine a suspicious place, scratch at it with his fingernail, or hold it up to the light. Oh, those 'inexpressibles' (as he called them), that let the sky's azure shine through at the knee, his inexpressibles, inexpressibly spiritualized by that ascension!

His room was characterized by the naive neatness of poverty. He would imprint his address and telephone number on his letters with a rubber stamp (a rubber stamp!). He knew how to make *botviniya*, a cold soup of beet tops. He was capable of demonstrating for hours on end some little trinket he considered a work of genius, a curious cuff link or cigarette lighter sold to him by a smooth-talking hawker (note that L. I. himself did not smoke), or his pets, three diminutive turtles with hideous cronelike necks; one of them perished in my presence when it crashed down from a round table along the edge of which it used to keep moving, like a hurrying cripple, under the impression that it was following a straight course, leading far, far away. Another thing that I just remembered with such clarity: on

98

the wall above his bed, which was as smooth as a prisoner's cot, hung two lithographs: a view of the Neva from the Columna Rostrata side and a portrait of Alexander I. He had happened to acquire them in a moment of yearning for the Empire, a nostalgia he distinguished from the yearning for one's native land.

L. I. totally lacked any sense of humor, and was totally indifferent to art, literature, and what is commonly known as nature. If the talk did happen to turn, say, to poetry, his contribution would be limited to a statement like 'No, say what you will, but Lermontov is somehow closer to us than Pushkin.' And when I pestered him to quote even a single line of Lermontov, he made an obvious effort to recall something out of Rubinstein's opera *The Demon*, or else answered, 'Haven't reread him in a long while, "all these are deeds of bygone days,"' and, anyway, my dear Victor, just let me alone.' Incidentally, he did not realize that he was quoting from Pushkin's *Ruslan and Ludmila*.

In the summer, on Sundays, he would invariably go on a trip out of town. He knew the outskirts of Berlin in astonishing detail and prided himself on his knowledge of 'wonderful spots' unfamiliar to others. This was a pure, self-sufficient delight, related, perhaps, to the delights of collectors, to the orgies indulged in by amateurs of old catalogues; otherwise it was incomprehensible why he needed it all: painstakingly preparing the rote, juggling various means of transportation (there by train, then back to this point by steamer, thence by bus, and this is how much it costs, and nobody, not even the Germans themselves, knows it is so cheap). But when he and I finally stood in the woods it turned out that he could not tell the difference between a bee and a bumblebee, or between alder and hazel, and perceived his surroundings quite conventionally and collectively: greenery, fine weather, the feathered tribe, little bugs. He was even offended if I, who had grown up in the country, remarked, for the sake of a bit of fun, on the differences between the flora around us and a forest in central Russia: he felt that there existed no significant difference, and that sentimental associations alone mattered.

He liked to stretch out on the grass in a shady spot, prop himself up on his right elbow, and discourse lengthily on the international situation or tell stories about his brother Peter, apparently quite a dashing fellow – ladies' man, musician, brawler – who, back in prehistoric times, drowned one summer night in the Dnieper – a very glamorous end. In dear old L. I.'s account, though, it all turned out so dull, so thorough, so well rounded out, that when, during a rest in the woods, he would suddenly ask with a kind smile, 'Did I ever tell you about the time Pete took a ride on the village priest's she-goat?' I felt like crying out, 'Yes, yes, you did, please spare me!'

What would I not give to hear his uninteresting yarns now, to see his absentminded, kindly eyes, that bald pate, rosy from the heat, those graying temples. What, then, was the secret of his charm, if everything about him was so dull? Why was everybody so fond of him, why did they all cling to him? What did he do in order to be so well liked? I don't know. I don't know the answer. I only know that I felt uneasy during his morning absences when he would leave for his Institute of Social Sciences (where he spent the time poring over bound volumes of *Die Ökonomische Welt*, from which he would copy in a neat, minute hand, excerpts that in his opinion were significant and noteworthy in the utmost), or for a private lesson of Russian, which he eternally taught to an elderly couple and the elderly couple's son-in-law; his association with them led him to make many incorrect conclusions about the German way of life – on which the members of our intelligentsia (the most unobservant race in the world) consider themselves authorities. Yes, I would feel uneasy, as though I had a premonition of what has since happened to him in Prague: heart failure in the street. How happy he was, though, to get that job in Prague, how he beamed! I have an exceptionally clear recollection of the day we saw him off. Just think, a man gets the opportunity to lecture on his favorite subject! He left me a pile of old magazines (nothing grows old and dusty as fast as a Soviet magazine), his shoe trees (shoe trees were destined to pursue me), and a brand-new fountain pen (as a memento). He showed great concern for me as he left, and I know that afterwards, when our correspondence somehow wilted and ceased, and life again crashed into deep darkness – a darkness howling with thousands of voices, from which it is unlikely I will ever escape – L. I., I know, kept thinking about me, questioning people, and trying to help indirectly. He left on a beautiful summer day; tears welled persistently in the eyes of some of those seeing him off; a myopic Jewish girl with white gloves and a lorgnette brought a whole sheaf of poppies and cornflowers; L. I. inexpertly sniffed them, smiling. Did it occur to me that I might be seeing him for the last time?

Of course it did. That is exactly what occurred to me: yes, I am seeing you for the last time; this, in fact is what I always think, about everything, about everyone. My life is a perpetual good-bye to objects and people, that often do not pay the least attention to my bitter, brief, insane salutation.

MAJOR E. DE STEIN

'Elegy On The Death of Bingo Our Trench Dog'

Weep, weep, ye dwellers in the delvèd earth,
　　Ah, weep, ye watchers by the dismal shore
　　Of No Man's Land, for Bingo is no more;
He is no more, and well ye knew his worth,
　　For whom on bully-beefless days were kept
Rare bones by each according to his means,
　　And, while the Quartermaster-Sergeant slept,
The elusive pork was rescued from the beans.
　　He is no more and, impudently brave,
　　The loathly rats sit grinning on his grave.

Him mourn the grimy cooks and bombers ten,
　　The sentinels in lonely posts forlorn,
　　The fierce patrols with hands and tunics torn,
The furtive band of sanitary men.
　　The murmuring sound of grief along the length
Of traversed trench the startled Hun could hear;
　　The Captain, as he struck him off the strength,
Let fall a sad and solitary tear;
　　'Tis even said a batman passing by
　　Had seen the Sergeant-Major wipe his eye.

The fearful fervour of the feline chase
　　He never knew, poor dog, he never knew;

Content with optimistic zeal to woo
Reluctant rodents in this murky place,
   He never played with children on clean grass,
Nor dozed at ease beside the glowing embers,
   Nor watched with hopeful eye the tea-cakes pass,
Nor smelt the heather-smell of Scotch Septembers,
   For he was born amid a world at war
   Athough unrecking what we struggled for.

Yet who shall say that Bingo was unblest
   Though all his Sprattless life was passed beneath
   The roar of mortars and the whistling breath
Of grim nocturnal heavies going West?
   Unmoved he heard the evening hymn of hate,
Unmoved would gaze into his master's eyes,
   For all the sorrows men for men create
In search of happiness wise dogs despise,
   Finding ecstatic joy in every rag
   And every smile of friendship worth a wag.

WILLIAM (JOHNSON) CORY

'Heraclitus'

They told me, Heraclitus, they told me you were dead,
They brought me bitter news to hear and bitter tears to shed.
I wept as I remember'd how often you and I
Had tired the sun with talking and sent him down the sky.
And now that thou art lying, my dear old Carian guest,
A handful of grey ashes, long, long ago at rest,
Still are thy pleasant voices, thy nightingales, awake;
For Death, he taketh all away, but them he cannot take.

ELSPETH SANDYS

from *Finding Out*

Braeside, Ron Anderson's farm, took in an area of over eight hundred acres, not all of which, despite the years of effort, was under cultivation. In the deep, sunless gullies the bush was still untouched. Only when a sheep went astray did Ron venture into the tangle of manuka, gorse and fern. Once the sheep was found and the break in the fence mended, the gully would revert to its original condition, accessible only to creatures small enough to penetrate its defences.

Ron would have been astonished if he'd known his daughter regularly found her way into one of the most remote of these gullies. Almost every day for the last four years Jennie had set off across the paddocks towards the gully that separated Braeside from the tribal lands of the southern headland. Reaching the gully she would pull up the wire fence, crawl through the gap, then navigate her way carefully through a break in the foliage. A few minutes later she would emerge in an open space surrounded on all sides by bush.

Jennie had found this 'secret place', as she called it, not long after her eighth birthday. Colin had inveigled her into joining him on a bird-nesting expedition. Though she loved the look and feel of the tiny speckled eggs, it had felt wrong to take them from their miraculously constructed nests. But pleasing Colin, then as now, mattered more to her than speaking her mind. So she became a thief for a day, and was rewarded by the discovery of a place that was to become her sanctuary against the world.

At first Jennie kept the knowledge of her hideaway to herself. The gully that concealed her secret was only a short walk from the track that led to the school. This meant she could easily make a detour on her way home in the afternoons. There was never any danger of Colin discovering her. Within a year of their bird-nesting expedition he had started at the Boys' High School in the city, so he no longer walked home across the paddocks. But even if he had, he wouldn't have been interested in anything she was doing.

The first thing Jennie did after making her discovery was construct a house. It required a considerable degree of subterfuge to smuggle the blankets, boxes and water-proof sheeting from the farm up to the gully. Having always regarded herself as a 'good' girl she was surprised how easy it was to be deceitful. When her mother first noticed a blanket missing, she was able, with very little compunction, to join in the search, shaking her head in wonder that so large an object could go astray.

Eventually the house was ready. It had timber walls tied together with twine and a roof of looped branches over which she had placed a tarpaulin. It wasn't always dry inside, but on warm days it was as cosy as her room at home. There were even flowers, when she could find them, squashed into a jam jar on the packing-case table. Windows she had dispensed with. What mattered was privacy. If she wanted to look out she could pull back the 'door' and gaze across the few remaining feet of open space at the bush.

Strangely enough, although she was more than a mile from the sea, she could hear it as if it were lapping just yards from her feet. She thought this must be because of the absence of other sounds. Protected as she was by the steep, densely bushed slopes on either side of the gully, she could hear nothing of the town. Only the water 'breathing' (how else could she explain the regular rise and fall of the waves?) and the gulls crying reached her in her eyrie. And occasionally, mournfully, the hoot of a ship's horn.

Sometimes, sitting in her makeshift house, Jennie felt sad. The noises from the sea suggested to her some vast universal sorrow linking all the countries and creatures of the world. She had the same feeling on the nights her mother played the piano. She had no idea why the sweet sounds drifting down the passage to her bedroom should so affect her, unless it was because she feared her mother must be sad too. Her mother only played the piano on the nights Jennie's father was out.

When she wasn't feeling sad, Jennie used the secret place to act out scenes of revenge or reconciliation with whoever happened to be her current enemy. Usually these scenes involved a passionate plea for forgiveness from her brother. Colin's treatment of his sister was not so much hostile as indifferent. Occasionally he would lower himself to notice her. (Once – a never-to-be-forgotten moment – he showed signs of distress when she choked on a piece of meat.) But mostly he brushed her off, physically as well as verbally, only really engaging with her when she'd been praised by one or both parents for her work at school. Those were the times Jennie hated most. Colin would call her a 'creep', and taunt her with the prospect of being a teacher herself one day, with not a friend in the world. Her only comfort then was to act out a scene in which she rescued Colin from drowning, or contracted a fatal disease. Either of these events she was confident would produce that longed-for look of love on her brother's face. Once she'd recreated that, her misery evaporated.

The decision to share her house with a real person rather than an imaginary one came about as a result of what Jennie later swore was a miracle. She'd been enduring one of her periodic bouts of unpopularity at school. She blamed these on her teachers, who persisted in making an example of her in front of the class. It didn't matter that she was held up as someone to emulate. – 'Don't just listen when Jennie reads, watch! See how she looks up from the book every few seconds. That's what you should all be doing. Letting your eye travel ahead.' – What mattered was that she was singled out.

On this particular occasion Jennie had been ostracized by her classmates for more than three weeks. The move against her was led by a newcomer to the school, Beverley Prendergast. When Jennie first realized how much Beverley hated her she was devastated, and full of self-pity. What had she done to deserve such hate? But as the days crept by, and there was no break in the wall of enmity surrounding her, she began to feel almost proud of her isolation. In her secret place she had books, a mouth organ, and the freedom to shout aloud if she wanted. Why should she envy Beverley, who only had a hoard of whispering cronies for company?

It was Mary Begg who broke the spell. On that day that was to change so much, Mary suddenly took it into her head to leave Beverley's pointing, giggling band of disciples and walk across the playground to join Jennie, who was standing by the fence trying to look inconspicuous. Jennie couldn't believe her eyes. She'd never paid much attention to Mary before. Their parents were friends, but that was more a reason to ignore her than seek her out. On that point, at least, she and Colin were in agreement. Having to team up with the children of their parents' friends was a recipe for disaster.

'Want to play hopscotch?' was Mary's opening remark.

'What?'

'Hopscotch. I've got some chalk.'

'You mean, you and me?'

'Who else?'

Jennie, glancing round at her enemies, saw a dozen pairs of eyes, staring fixedly. 'What about them?'

'Who's scared of them?'

'I am,' Jennie admitted.

Mary flicked her plaits behind her shoulders, a magnificent gesture Jennie thought at the time. 'They don't scare me a bit,' she boasted.

That had been the start of it. Later they walked home together. 'Got something to show you,' Jennie said, when she judged herself safe from school and its torments. 'It's a secret.'

'What sort of secret?'

'The best kind. Magic. You know.'

Mary appeared to give this some thought, then she said, 'You're a funny girl, Jennie Anderson. Is it 'cos you're brainy?'

'I'm not brainy a bit,' Jennie denied hotly. 'You don't want to believe everything Beverley Prendergast says.'

Once Mary had seen the secret place, the friendship was sealed. As the years went by, and the house slowly filled with improvised furnishings, Jennie and Mary came to acknowledge it as the place where they were most happy. No other location, not even on holidays, could bestow that special mixture of thrill and safety. It was where they went to complain about parents, brothers, and friends who weren't 'best' but featured, nevertheless, in their dramas.

For Jennie, who had never had a best friend before, it was the start of the happiest time of her life. Once inside the house, she and Mary would listen to the sea and dream aloud of the lives they would lead when they were grown up. Not for them the drudgery of suburban marriage and motherhood. They saw themselves in exotic places, beloved of exciting, handsome men. (Mary always chose a soldier, Jennie a concert pianist.) What exactly this loving involved they were careful not to specify. Jennie, being a farm girl, knew the facts of life, but she couldn't equate these with the sense of mystery and delight she felt certain, from her reading and her own over-active imagination, were what loving was really about. The trouble was, no one ever talked about it. The subject was as taboo as devil-worship or cannibalism.

On the day of the new schoolteacher's arrival Jennie and Mary had gone to their house as usual. Mary was expected home early, so they could only spend a brief time there. But the excitement and relief they'd felt at the departure of Mrs Slatter had to be expressed.

'Sheepface! Cow-tits hanging down to her knees! Pig's eyes!' Mary screamed.

'Dragon! Tartar! Fire-eater!' Jennie countered, her mind full of pictures of a circus she'd once been taken to. 'Next time she uses that strap I hope . . .' She caught her breath in a paroxysm of imagined revenge. 'Hope a tiger gobbles her up.'

'She's like the Wicked Queen in *Snow White*, isn't she? Only she's ugly.'

'I suppose she's not *all* bad,' Jennie acknowledged, remembering, suddenly, the look on Mrs Slatter's face as her pupils shuffled up to say goodbye. 'I mean, not what you'd call *wicked*.'

'She was pretty wicked to Albert Jackson.'

Jennie was silent. Albert Jackson held the school record for being strapped. Three times a week, on average; and on one fateful day, three times in one morning. Albert was not only stupid, he was an orphan, a fatal combination in Mrs Slatter's eyes. Yet he never did anything really bad, not that Jennie could see. He sniffed a lot, and sometimes laughed for no reason at all. Once, shatteringly, he wet his pants in front of the whole class. He'd been standing on a chair in a corner of the classroom – punishment for some now-forgotten crime – when suddenly there was a rush of water, and a loud gasp from those seated nearest him. The next moment Mrs Slatter yanked him off his chair and hurled him out of the room. For days afterwards a debate raged as to whether Albert had committed this act of sacrilege deliberately. Jennie secretly hoped he had. it would mean he was not victim but rebel.

Mary kicked off her shoes and flopped down on the pile of sacks and stolen blankets that did duty for a bed. 'What d'ya

110

reckon he'll be like, this new teacher? Dad says he's twenty-nine.'

'Old. Pity.'

'I think older men are better. More romantic.'

'You've been reading that book I lent you.'

'"He looked at her long and hard,"' Mary quoted. '"Could she really be so young? Was it possible he was falling in love with a mere slip of a girl?"'

Jennie ran her hands over her belly. 'No one would ever call *me* that,' she said crossly.

'Anyway we'll see him tomorrow.' Mary sat up and hugged her knees.

'It's Saturday,' Jennie reminded.

'The social, nitwit! You are coming, aren't you?'

'I hate socials. I hate everything that happens in that smelly old hall.'

'About all that ever does happen round here,' Mary pointed out amiably. 'So you'd better stop moaning.'

'Colin will go out the back and drink beer, and Dad will have a fit, and Mum will try to pretend nothing's happened.'

'My mum and dad will spend all their time dancing with each other.'

Jennie cast a furtive glance at her friend. Mr and Mrs Begg were famous for their devotion. But it just wasn't possible to think of them 'in love', the way people were in books.

'Colin's going out with Avril Prendergast,' Mary announced. 'Did you know?'

Jennie felt her heart turn over.

'Beverley saw them when they got off the bus. He was kissing her and kissing her. Beverley said she saw him put his hand inside her blouse.'

'I don't believe you. He wouldn't. Not in front of all those people.'

'Beverley said it was a dare.'

'Well then.'

Mary flopped back on the bed. 'He's quite good looking, your brother. In a spotty sort of way.'

'He is not spotty.'

'Suit yourself.'

Jennie turned her face away. What she thought about Colin couldn't be shared, not even with her best friend. The thought that he might be the sort of boy she occasionally heard her parents whispering about was too terrible to put into words. 'Do we *have* to go to this social?' she asked plaintively.

'Won't your parents make you?'

'If we didn't go you could come and stay at my house. I'm sure Mum would let you.'

Mary pushed her lips through a sequence of shapes. 'Well I want to go,' she said. 'I want to see what Mr Matheson looks like.'

'If he's a schoolteacher he can't be anything special.'

'They're not all like Mrs Slatter.'

'Oh really? Name one who's different.'

'Well there was Miss Dent.'

'She was only there for a term.'

'She was pretty.'

'Exactly. So she got out, didn't she? Got married.'

'Mr McTaggart wasn't so bad.'

'Pooh!' Jennie dismissed the now retired standard three teacher with a wave of her hand. 'He was pathetic.'

It was an unsatisfactory conversation. Later, walking home across the paddocks, Jennie comforted herself with the thought that even best friends sometimes disagreed. But the unease remained. Mary's interest in Saturday night's social was something new. The real world had conjured up a rival magic.

W. H. DAVIES

'A Child's Pet'

When I sailed out of Baltimore
  With twice a thousand head of sheep,
They would not eat, they would not drink,
  But bleated o'er the deep.

Inside the pens we crawled each day,
  To sort the living from the dead;
And when we reached the Mersey's mouth,
  Had lost five hundred head.

Yet every night and day one sheep,
  That had no fear of man or sea,
Stuck through the bars its pleading face,
  And it was stroked by me.

And to the sheep-men standing near,
  'You see,' I said, 'this one tame sheep:
It seems a child has lost her pet,
  And cried herself to sleep.'

So every time we passed it by,
  Sailing to England's slaughter-house,
Eight ragged sheep-men – tramps and thieves –
  Would stroke that sheep's black nose.

FLEUR ADCOCK

'A Hymn to Friendship'

Somehow we manage it: to like our friends,
to tolerate not only their little ways
but their huge neuroses, their monumental oddness:
'Oh well', we smile, 'it's one of his funny days.'

Families, of course, are traditionally awful:
embarrassing parents, ghastly brothers, mad aunts
provide a useful training-ground to prepare us
for the pseudo-relations we acquire by chance.

Why them, though? Why not the woman in the library
(grey hair, big mouth) who reminds us so of J?
Or the one on Budgen's delicatessen counter
(shy smile, big nose) who strongly resembles K?

— Just as the stout, untidy gent on the train
reading *The Mail on Sunday* through pebble specs
could, with somewhat sparser hair and a change
of reading-matter, be our good friend X.

True, he isn't; they aren't; but why does it matter?
Wouldn't they do as well as the friends we made
in the casual past, by being at school with them,
or living next door, or learning the same trade?

Well, no, they wouldn't. Imagine sharing a tent
with one of these look-alikes, and finding she snored:
no go. Or listening for days on end while she dithered
about her appalling marriage: we'd be bored.

Do we feel at all inclined to lend them money?
Or travel across a continent to stay
for a weekend with them? Or see them through an abortion,
a divorce, a gruelling court-case? No way.

Let one of these impostors desert his wife
for a twenty-year-old, then rave all night about
her sensitivity and her gleaming thighs,
while guzzling all our whisky: we'd boot him out.

And as for us, could we ring them up at midnight
when our man walked out on us, or our roof fell in?
Would they offer to pay our fare across the Atlantic
to visit them? The chances are pretty thin.

Would they forgive our not admiring their novel,
or saying we couldn't really take to their child,
or confessing that years ago we went to bed
with their husband? No, they wouldn't: they'd go wild.

Some things kindly strangers will put up with,
but we need to know exactly what they are:
it's OK to break a glass, if we replace it,
but we mustn't let our kids be sick in their car.

Safer to stick with people who remember
how we ourselves, when we and they were nineteen,
threw up towards the end of a student party
on ethyl alcohol punch and methedrine.

In some ways we've improved since then. In others
(we glance at the heavy jowls and thinning hair,
hoping we're slightly better preserved than they are)
at least it's a deterioration we share.

It can't be true to say that we chose our friends,
or surely we'd have gone for a different lot,
while they, confronted with us, might well have decided
that since it was up to them they'd rather not.

But something keeps us hooked, now we're together,
a link we're not so daft as to disparage –
nearly as strong as blood-relationship
and far more permanent, thank God, than marriage.

NANN MORGENSTERN

The Befriender

'Chuck that down the sink, would you?' Frances handed me a plastic bottle filled with fluorescent orange sludge.

There was a sink a few feet away from Frances's bed, although the hospice room also had its own *en suite* bathroom.

'What the hell is it – drain cleaner?' I snorted as the fizzy mixture gurgled down the plughole.

Frances laughed. 'Martha's Special Brew: carrot juice and wheat grass. She makes it herself and brings me some every day. I can't stomach it. No, don't throw away the bottle, she'll be wanting it back.'

Martha was some middle-aged bag with an eerie beneficent smile who hovered ever more frequently in the wings of Frances's fast-fading life. They'd met a few months ago, last time Frances had been given a holiday from the hospice and had hobbled to her local church to give thanks, I guess, for yet another reprieve. Never previously a frequent churchgoer, Frances found increasing solace in, if not religion, the quiet stability of her Camden Town parish. Martha, seemingly, came attached, and who was I to complain as she unhesitatingly took up the slack that the summer season and the kids at home created for Laura and me in terms of visiting rotas. This is not to say that Laura and I were not ourselves middle-aged bags, but because we'd all met a decade or so earlier in our thirties, we still saw one another as we once used to be: Laura, an aristocratic hippie; Frances, a droll northerner with an individualistic, almost Sitwellian style and myself, a straight-toothed American with a grin that made me look like Alfred E. Neuman from *Mad Magazine*, so they said. None of us would dream of dressing Martha-style in polyester tracksuits with stripes down the side and foot-straps combined with dressy-looking but scuffed flat black pumps with bows on the toes.

'I hope they're going to spring me again,' Frances said almost shyly. 'I'm feeling OK, loads stronger, and the weather's so great. What I really want to do is to be home for my birthday, maybe have a party like the old times, invite a few of the Old Buggers and other odds and sods. Dunc phoned last night and said he'll definitely be coming over. It'll be great – I haven't seen him in three years, not since Mother died.'

Duncan was Frances's research chemist brother who had lived in California for twelve years: the Primrose Hill flat was his. I'd never met him as he rarely returned to the UK, although he'd promised to visit ever since the cancer came back eighteen months ago.

Frances didn't look all that bright to me but, like Laura, I'd learned to take my cue from Frances. 'Sounds great,' I said, 'I don't believe I'm finally going to meet the big hunk in person.'

'Don't hold your breath,' Frances laughed as Martha clomped into the room. Duncan was as famous for his unkept promises as he was for his six-foot-four good looks.

'Morning, sunshine,' Martha beamed. 'You're looking like the cat who's got the pigeon today. What's up?' She fished another container of her Special Brew from her string bag and placed it on Frances's bedside cupboard with the flourish of a magician anticipating a burst of applause.

'Yum,' Frances conceded. I handed Martha yesterday's bottle, which she flung into her bag as she sat down on the other visitor's chair.

118

'What's the excitement?' she asked, leaning forward already in anticipation.

'Frances's brother says he's coming over. Duncan, the research chemist, who lives in La Jolla,' I explained. Martha looked blank.

'You know, I told you about him. It's his flat I live in, remember?' Frances said impatiently. 'And I think they're going to let me go home while he's here, or at least that's what I'm aiming at.'

'That's wonderful, Frances, and will Duncan look after you?' Martha laughed.

'Pigs might fly, I suppose,' Frances answered her airily. 'I don't think he'd even change the sheets on my death bed. A joke . . .' she said at our aghast expressions.

'Ha,' I acknowledged. 'Look, I've got to pick the kids up in an hour and I still have to go to Safeway. Are you OK, you two?'

Frances nodded and Martha said, 'Of course, not to worry. I can stay until your other friend gets here, dear.'

I kissed Frances on the forehead gently and fled the room, trying not to look as glad to be going as I felt. Thank God for Martha, I thought, even though I couldn't stand being in the same room with her. Laura agreed, but we both felt mean as hell since the Befriender, as we called her, had such relentless good cheer and such an over-developed sense of responsibility that it lifted some of the burden of each from ourselves.

Laura and I had never been bosom pals before Frances's first bout of cancer. We'd occasionally all go to the cinema and have a meal together but mostly we would go out with Frances individually, catch up on the other's news via her, or would sit together at an Old Buggers session, musing drunkenly about politics, life and the ever-elusive Zipless Fuck. I'd overlapped with Frances at the Travel Bug. She'd been there about a year, her two VSO years in Ghana and the Bahamas having persuaded her that travelling, sort of, rather than teaching was her bag. I'd come over from New

York, newly married to a Brit but unqualified, both for a job and, as it turned out, for marriage itself. My post-grad eighteen months in the Peace Corps in Venezuela and what sounded like fluent Spanish eventually won me the chance to be trained by Frances on the long-haul desk of the TB. Two years after I left for an editorial job at a publisher of travel guides, Laura landed a job at the Travel Bug, her embassy-hopping childhood at last standing her in good stead. It was Laura's first job, although like us she was in her mid-thirties and, like me, divorced with two young boys.

Frances was the only woman of our age Laura and I knew who had never been married – not even tempted to be, who went to her local and just drank and joked, as foul-mouthed as any of the lads, who treated her with almost as much respect as she naturally commanded. She was no one's 'old lady', though she shared her bed on an irregular basis with Sandy, whose nature was as feck-free as his boyish name and whose own 'old lady' in Kentish Town was never once glimpsed at the Horticultural. Sandy was Duncan's best mate from back when and Frances seemed to have inherited him with the flat, but a total lack of any bone in his body except his elbow (and his trousers, if Frances could be believed) made Laura and me dismiss him as That Sot rather than anyone who could be remotely relied upon as Frances became increasingly frail.

I phoned Laura at nine thirty that night, after I was sure she'd got back from the hospice and had collected and fed her kids. Frances had been given the go-ahead to go home the following morning: she'd given her keys to Martha, who had volunteered to clean and air the flat and do a major shop before collecting her at eleven. Laura sounded a bit put out.

'Tim and Dom are off to Windsor Safari Park with Ben tomorrow, so I could easily have brought Frances home and stayed with her all day, but Martha'd made all the arrangements with Matron before I even got there today.'

'She is a bit much,' I agreed. 'And, frankly, I don't think Frances is in any fit state to be going home, with or without Martha or that nurse who came last time. God, she can hardly stand up or walk to the loo. What about her front stairs? Look, I think we've both got to be there to help.'

'Martha's organized an orderly or someone, wouldn't you know?'

We arranged to meet at Frances's flat before she arrived.

'I've got loads of veggie lasagne in the freezer,' I told her. 'I'll bring some over. Thank God it's Saturday and Will and Stephanie'll have the boys until bedtime Sunday.'

'Listen, do you agree: I think one of us will have to phone Duncan. I want to know if he's actually going to get his arse over here this time.'

'Yup, why don't you?' I said. 'I don't like this at all. It just seems out of control. There's no way she can stay in that flat on her own.'

'Frances is absolutely adamant. I tried to argue with her, but she's made up her mind. She wants to go home, even if it's for one last time, and Martha's not helping at all to discourage her,' Laura sighed.

I sighed, too. 'Make sure Duncan knows and appreciates what's happening. I mean, that Frances is worse, not better. He may have got the wrong message from her.'

'Even if I have to go over there and drag him back with me, I'll make sure he comes this time,' Laura promised.

'I had to leave a message on Duncan's machine, sod him,' Laura said when we met at Frances's flat in the morning. 'I asked him to phone here, if he couldn't get me at home.'

The flat was spotless and smelled fresh. Martha had even put out a jug of Frances's favourite flower, ranunculus, on the coffee table. There was a light flashing on Frances's answer phone. It had to be Duncan, we agreed silently, and Laura played the message. It was: he was flying out on Friday, sorry about that, but he just couldn't get away any earlier. He'd phone Frances in the morning. I hit the erase button savagely. 'Fuck him, fuck him, fuck him!'

'Look, you've got a reception committee!' Martha shouted over her shoulder as she hefted Frances's case through to the sitting-room. Frances followed in the arms of a burly young man, tiny and yellowy-pale on this sunny summer day, buttoned up tightly in her gorgeous gaudy faux-leopard coat which I'd always coveted.

'I'm Brian. Morning, ladies,' he nodded in our direction as he set Frances gently on the sofa bed.

She lay back, sighing contentedly, 'Home!'

'Thank you so much, Brian,' Martha said. 'Do you want a cuppa before you go back?'

'Just let me fetch that wheelchair from the van. I don't have to be back until twelve fifteen, so there's just time.'

We watched him leap up Frances's steep wooden front steps three at a time.

'Wouldn't you rather be in bed, dear?' Martha shouted from the kitchen. 'There's fresh sheets on it.'

'No, thanks. There's time enough for that.' Frances struggled to a sitting position. I tried to help her out of her coat, but she batted me away. 'I'm absolutely freezing,' she said. 'Can you bear to put the heating on?'

Laura and I looked at each other under raised eyebrows. The day was well into the eighties and Frances's basement flat wasn't that much cooler.

I went into the kitchen and fiddled with the boiler timer. Electronics are not my forte.

'We've got one just like that at home. I'll do it. She's bound to want it on all the time now – she's so thin,' Martha said.

I left her to it and took the tea tray in as Brian bounded through the sitting-room doorway and Frances was saying, 'Fuck him, fuck him,' into a crumpled tissue.

Laura and I said, 'You can say that again.'

I helped Brian to a cup of tea, which he milked and sugared and bolted down, obviously realizing he'd come back in at an emotional moment. 'Sorry, ladies, got to go. Need some instructions on how to fold up that chair?'

We shook our heads, all by now used to the chair routine after Frances had almost ceased using her fabulous antique malacca cane that Laura and I had come across in Camden Passage last summer. Like Frances, it had real style and it seemed to dignify her condition.

'Thanks again, Brian,' Frances wiped her nose. 'See you.' She blew weakly into her tea.

Martha let Brian out. 'It'll be toasty soon, Frances. Well, I'll leave you three to it for now. I'll give you a tinkle around four to see if there's anything you want or need.'

'You'd better keep those,' Frances told her as she laid the keys on the coffee table. 'I won't be needing them myself, I don't think.'

'Yes, well . . .' Martha slipped the keys back into her bag and left.

Frances pointed to the wheelchair. 'I'm dying to see my garden. Hope all my beauties are still alive.'

Frances's patio was a miracle of blossom. Flo upstairs had been aiming her hose at it from her kitchen window every now and then. She'd also been looking after Tyrone, Frances's cat, who now butted and rubbed himself along the wheels of the chair. I deadheaded a few roses as Laura switched on the pump for the subtle water trough Sandy had installed two summers ago in an aberrantly altruistic moment. Frances sighed out of pure content and stretched her faux-leopard arms up to the sun. 'I feel wonderful,' she stated. 'What the hell . . .'

Frances had a long nap in bed after lunch. Laura and I organized a rota, writing in Martha's name with a question mark beside it until we checked with her when she phoned. With a bit of kid-shifting, Laura's to spend the night with me and vice versa with Martha spelling us, we could actually manage round-the-clock care until Duncan arrived. Flo upstairs said she'd do anything we needed as well, and Martha had already arranged for a daily nurse to bath

Frances and change her dressings. We were high with the relief of actually figuring out how to cope: I would stay tonight, Martha said she could stay tomorrow. I'd have Laura's boys Monday and she'd stay with Frances that night and so on, with Martha, who I think was a widow, doing day duty.

Frances awoke in an equally high mood and, in spite of having to take her pain pills twice, busied us organizing the party for some of the Old Buggers and the Horticultural set for the following Saturday night over the vegetarian lasagne and a bottle of red. Laura and I got Frances to bed by eight thirty and finished off the bottle, and she went home to Dom and Tim.

Duncan phoned the next morning. It was one a.m. in California and he sounded pretty much the worse for wear. Frances was still asleep and too bleary when I woke her to muster the energy to demand he come any earlier than Friday.

'Doesn't the bastard realize I'm dying?' she muttered to me as she replaced the receiver on the phone I held out to her, the cord just that bit too short to reach the bed. I'd have to get some sort of extension lead, I was thinking, and not focusing on what Frances had said until after she'd said it. Laura and I hadn't been certain that Frances actually acknowledged how much more ill she was this time.

I put the phone on the floor and hugged her gently, afraid she might break into bits. She hugged me back for a long silent time. I could hear the hypnotic sound of the water splashing in the trough outside. We'd forgotten to turn it off the day before.

Martha came at noon as promised, just as Amelia, the nurse, was finishing with Frances. I apologized for the way Duncan's non-appearance was disrupting her life.

Martha said, 'Nonsense. I gather he's something of a pig.'

'A right bastard,' I said, warming to her.

Frances was wearing a skirt and roll-neck jumper, both obviously much too large for her and too wintry for the blazing day. She was determined to get out of the flat and happily agreed to go with Martha to Evensong if she still felt up to it later on. We all had coffee on the patio and I left Frances with Martha after we installed the phone and Frances's address book beside her. She wanted to invite people to her birthday party herself. Flo would help Martha with the chair before and after church and I would drop by later to cook supper before Will and Stephanie returned the boys.

What with Martha and the morphine, the next couple of days passed easily enough, although Laura and I could hardly bear the courage with which Frances went about the remains of her life. We got by through not talking about it and by fooling ourselves that Duncan's arrival and the birthday party were actually going to happen. We menu-planned, ordered the wine and beer to be delivered, and for Duncan we all three trundled out to buy a new sofa bed – as Frances's old one was pretty crocked – although Laura and I, in one of our now rare moments of frankness, agreed that the purchase was optimistic in the extreme. Frances had worried away at the thought until I simply had to organize going in to work late on Wednesday and run her down to a place on the Tottenham Court Road. We picked out an inoffensive beige job, which the manager accommodatingly promised to deliver the next morning, and take away the clapped-out old one free, no sweat. If they failed to deliver the sofa, we still had a day to remedy the situation before Duncan's arrival.

According to Martha and Flo, who were detailed to oversee the changeover, the delivery men spent a good two hours huffing and puffing, but nothing could shrink the new sofa to the measurements required to get it down the stairs of Frances's basement area and totally into the flat. Frances was distraught and the only solution she would accept was that the men left the new sofa propped up vertically against the inside porch wall inside its plastic bubble wrap coat. As there was now only a foot or so of space left for anything to get by the looming bulk of the expensive, new useless thing, the delivery men left the shabby old sofa in the sitting-room. Duncan, the giant of brain and brawn, would fix it, Frances had cried hoarsely, the veins popping on her forehead, a frightened Martha whispered to me on the phone. Martha had had to get her to bed right away and soothe her in the dark for an hour or so, she reported later.

Duncan phoned that night when I was there. Frances was too tired to be more than phlegmatic when he said he was too tied up at the lab trying to meet a deadline to be able to make it to London before next Wednesday at the very earliest, sorry to miss her birthday and all that. All the life had gone out of her by the time she hung up the receiver.

I rang the Horticultural in despair. It was only a few yards down the road, but I didn't want to leave Frances alone for even a minute. Sandy arrived within a half hour, a half-full bottle of Bells in tow: only he could cheer her up. He carried her into the bedroom, came out to retrieve the whisky and then fortunately spent most of the night with her. To the sounds of their whispered laughter, I grimly put new sheets on the old sofa bed.

The next two days were bad. Frances was exhausted and in more pain. She spent much of her time in bed. Although Laura and I pleaded with her, she refused to cancel the party. Martha made sausage rolls and Scotch eggs. We thanked her for her offerings: it took all our energy just to buy and open a few bags of crisps, toss a lame salad and set out the drink. Flo made a chocolate cake, which she silently handed me at the front door, saying she wouldn't stay but have a grand time anyway. Laura and I had both forgotten about a cake along with the rest of our potential gourmet menu. Martha, Laura and I planned another rota for the week, this time discounting Duncan's proposed Wednesday arrival. Martha said she wouldn't stay for the party either. I was disappointed and I think possibly Laura was too: it was going to be an ordeal greeting fresh-faced friends who hadn't seen Frances for a while and who, we knew, would not be able to hide their shock at her deterioration. Martha insisted she wasn't good with a load of strangers, but not to worry, she'd definitely be back bright and early in the morning to help with the clearing up.

Laura turned on Capital Radio for some loudness and cheer, even if false. I set about arranging Frances's favourite antique shawl into an artful turban, which I fastened with the jet brooch which matched her most extravagantly long bead earrings, while Frances directed Laura to find the tapes she wanted to be played throughout the evening. We'd ironed the dress Frances wanted to wear earlier in the day, but when the time came she said she was just too shagged to change so I draped a few more shawls and scarves round her on the sofa, where she would hold court. Laura smudged some green shadow on Frances's lids, which made her look terrible but we couldn't admit that to her. We daubed some away with tissues and spit as subtly as we could.

I don't know about Laura, but I was well on my way to being pissed by the time the first lot of Old Buggers arrived, loudly joking about the excess of sofas as they jostled their way into the sitting-room. I hope Frances didn't see the succession of shocked stares; if she did, she didn't seem to mind, continuing to sip at her goblet of red wine and reminiscing with the best of them. Most of the Horticultural lot settled on the patio, but Sandy stayed with Frances on the sofa. It was far too hot to dance, even though Laura had remembered to turn the heat off, but with everyone crashed out in a loose circle round the walls and Simeon, known to us as Marianne Faithless, regaling us with his latest trolley dolly folly, it could almost have been any reunion over the years. I relaxed and Laura laughed loudly, even though she whispered to me that she heard Simeon's story at least ten times a day at work. We both smiled at each other and toasted ourselves, happy that Frances had gone through with the birthday event.

Just after nine or so I went in to the kitchen to cut the cake. I was arranging portions on paper plates when Sandy came in.

'I think she's had enough now, really. I don't want to frighten you, but her eyes are sort of rolling back in her head. Her last tablet didn't work and she's looking, well, like death, really.'

My heart leapt into my throat. I hoped to God she wasn't going to have one of those truly awful fits. Shoving a couple of plates at Sandy, I went to Frances. Laura was leaning over her, urging her to lie down and rearranging her turban, which had slipped down. Anxious friends crowded round the sofa.

'Come on, folks, time to go home. The birthday girl definitely needs her beauty sleep.' Within minutes Sandy shooed out all the guests, who left in relative silence, some surprised by having paper plates of cake shoved into their nervous hands.

Sandy carried Frances into the bedroom and laid her gently on the bed. 'I'm sorry, I'm sorry,' she whispered over and over. Sandy removed her turban and lay down next to her, whispering to us, 'I think she just needs to sleep. I'll stay with her,' as we hovered anxiously in the doorway.

Laura and I mutely removed to the sitting-room and debated phoning a doctor or ambulance. We huddled together on the sofa amid the party debris, Joan Armatrading's voice still giving the flat a semblance of life.

Sandy woke us at about four in the morning. Frances was asleep, her breathing sounded even and okay and he just had to get home or all hell would break loose. He'd be back in the morning. We had opened out the sofa bed and had been lying on it stiffly, afraid and far too keyed up to sleep for more than a few minutes at a time.

We spent the rest of the night creeping about the flat, looking in on Frances every few minutes while clearing up the flat and patio, alternating cups of coffee with the dregs of abandoned glasses, feeling helpless.

Frances was still asleep when the nurse arrived. Martha let herself in five minutes later, while we were all in the bedroom, the nurse gently trying to rouse Frances.

'She should go back to Heathervale now, you know. It's time. I think she should know this.'

The ambulance came about twenty minutes later. Martha had packed a small case with Frances's toilet bag and some nighties and a dressing gown. Frances, finally awake and not protesting, having drowsily directed her.

Martha put Frances's coat round her on the gurney. It was very difficult to get the stretcher past the sofa bed on the wall without either hurting Frances or tipping her sideways, but the ambulance men managed. The nurse left – nothing more for her to do. Martha volunteered to go with Frances in the ambulance as both Laura and I had to make unexpected arrangements for our children. We hugged Frances farewell. I phoned Flo about the cat and Sandy and Laura rang Duncan's number, leaving an urgent message on his machine. We locked up Frances's flat and drove separately to the hospice.

The hospice visiting regime, interrupted such a short time ago, resumed, Martha spending most days there with Laura and me coming whenever we could manage. Frances was rarely awake or fully coherent. Sandy didn't come to see Frances, though he did leave a message for her. Duncan sent flowers and told Matron on the phone he would be there Wednesday for sure.

Martha was already there and Laura and I were summoned separately that Wednesday by the hospice, who knew there was no time left. My unlucky assistant had taken the call at the office and tracked me down in a Thai restaurant with an author, whom I left in mid-meal to foot the bill, while I raced to Heathervale in a taxi – actually telling the driver to step on it.

Frances died in an armchair two hours later, surrounded and embraced by the three of us. Duncan arrived at the hospice three hours later, not knowing Frances was dead: Laura, Martha and I were still sitting in a side room, having been given pot after pot of tea by various compassionate nurses, crying, talking and sometimes laughing.

Duncan managed to get the sofa returned and refunded to Frances's account. He'd put the flat on the market and had been assured of a good, quick sale, he told us at the funeral. He said that Frances had left him a letter: Laura was to get Frances's jewellery; I, her antique shawls and handbags; Martha, her faux-leopard coat; and Sandy, her fancy French lingerie. I don't know if Sandy collected the underwear. We're not in touch. Laura and I see each other once or twice a year, mostly at Old Bugger gatherings. I think of Martha every time I see a faux-leopardskin coat on someone swinging up the street, above bad shoes.

ANGUS WILSON

Christmas Day in the Workhouse

Thea was showing one of the new girls how to mark the personnel cards when Major Prosser came in. She continued the demonstration without turning round, not because she thought the work of more importance than the Head of Section's visit, but because she guessed that his sense of his own position would be more flattered by assuming it so. After four years at the Bureau, actions tended to be guided by such purely personal considerations. Where all other values had been effaced by isolation and boredom, only sexual conquest or personal advantage remained as possible goals; most of the time Thea found only personal advantage within her range, but at a certain cost in hysteria she had made quite a success of it – she was, after all, the only woman head of a subsection under the age of thirty.

'Directed staff are marked green for sick leave, volunteers blue, established officers red,' she explained, as she looked at the new girl's pallid skin, she wondered if green had been purposely chosen for the conscripts. She tried very hard to treat these bewildered and unattractive girls with kindness. Sometimes, however, a bitter despair would break through the deadness with which she had insulated herself from the place, and in her anger at the naive enthusiasm with which *she* had first volunteered for the work, she would turn against those who had only come under duress. At such

131

times she would dwell with satisfaction upon these sickly suburban ewe lambs – green-faced girls with pebble glasses, protruding teeth and scurfy shoulders who had been hunted from the protecting parental arms to be sacrificed upon the pyre of communal existence. In fact, of course, as she fully realized, this monotony of ugliness was simply the ready response of the Ministry of Labour to the Bureau's call for 'clever girls'.

'For the dying, the dead, and those yet unborn, we use black,' she went on. It was a joke she had inherited from her predecessor who had thought it out way back in 1939, but as she made it she realized that it was not quite Tim Prosser's sort of remark. It reflected, if only faintly, a certain cynicism towards the Bureau which he preferred only to reserve for expansive moods with his immediate sub-ordinates. All the 'old faithfuls' among the girls laughed obediently, and Joan Fowler even managed to impart a special note of devotion towards Thea into her little giggle.

Major Prosser's laugh was really more of an impatient cough. He was beginning to see this devotion to work as *lèse-majesté* rather than a compliment.

'Have you got Braddock's card there?' he said abruptly. He always used the girls' surnames when he wished to wound the remnants of humane feelings to which Thea clung as the last plank of her self-respect.

'Daphne's card?' she replied on a lingering note, as she tried to puzzle out what he was after.

'Yes, yes,' Major Prosser was impatient. 'The girl with the migraines and the excess charm.' He liked Thea's competence, but he genuinely despised her gentility and what he called her 'blasted hard-boiled virginity.'

Anxious to oblige, the new girl handed the card to him directly. He gave her a friendly, boyish smile that reminded her of her daddy.

'Away since September,' he said sharply, 'I say, Thea, you ought to have asked me for a replacement ages ago.

132

Establishment's no sinecure at the best of times, but carrying passengers!' and he looked all admiration for her silent
self-sacrifice. 'Let's see, who can we give you? I know –
Turnbull. I'll see Room 6 straight away.'

My God! thought Thea, so that's it. As soon as he laid a
new wench – increasingly she found herself using the
'tough' language affected by her superiors – there was
always a shift round of staff. He'd put his new little bit in
charge of Room 6 and now he'd got to weed out the duds for
her. He would have his work cut out in finding a home for
Turnbull, whose black frizz with its bleached streak made
her absence from evening shift to have a bit of fun with the
messengers seem somehow more noticeable than in
'quieter' girls.

'Thank you, Tim,' said Thea sweetly. The constant use of
Christian names among the heads and sub-heads was one
of the many external signs of the splendid, amateur,
wartime spirit with which they were making rings round
the inflexible efficiency of the enemy, *and* having fun in
doing it. Though Thea had no doubts of the truth of this
claim to improvised genius, she often found its conscious
expression embarrassing. She was, however, rapidly learning the language by which modesty, reserve and reticence
can be widely advertised.

'Thank you, Tim, I don't think there'll be any need,' she
went on, 'Joan Fowler had a letter from Daphne saying she
would be back within a fortnight. That's right, isn't it,
Joan?'

Joan was so delighted that Thea should have turned to
her for support that she blushed wildly and her genteelly
distorted vowels tumbled over one another in an effort to
please.

'Oh, yes, Thea, she's ever so much better, really almost all
right, and her doctor says that as long . . .'

Major Prosser laughed to disguise his disgust at Joan's
lack of sex-appeal. 'That's not perhaps quite the official
report,' he said, 'in any case,' and he looked round the room

somewhat venomously, 'a drop of new blood might be a very good idea. We all get a bit stale, anaemic . . .'

But Thea was ready for such a favourite generalization, and quoted another of his loved phrases back at him.

'Except, Tim, that in Establishments we have a highly integrated group of specially picked personnel.' She knew the phrase from his last report to the chief. He took the joke against himself with a 'good sport' smile, but she could see he was getting angry.

'Well, we'll talk about it later,' he said.

Thea decided that the moment had come to push her victory home. 'I don't suppose it matters,' she said, 'but in the report I did for the Duce' – it was their jolly name for the chief, originally bestowed in bitter contempt, but wisely accepted by him as a piece of family fun – 'saying why the section needed more staff I did mention that we never cared to move people from one job to another.'

Major Prosser was already somewhat alarmed by the difficulties of justifying his request for forty new personnel – a request made because other sections were increasing – so that the blow was a telling one. Nevertheless, Thea reflected, she would probably have to put up with Turnbull's bleached streak, for unless she was prepared to make a row about it, Tim could always override her wishes.

'No Christmas decorations yet?' he asked, dismissing the matter.

'We're putting them up tomorrow morning,' said Thea. 'We've got some wonderful caricatures this year.'

'One of me, I hope,' said Tim.

'Well yes,' laughed Thea, 'show him what you've done, Stephanie.'

If Tim had been expecting giggles and a shy refusal, he was sadly disappointed. Stephanie ignored him altogether, but taking the drawing from a folder on her table, she handed it to Thea.

'I've got to colour the uniform still,' she remarked in her offhand, dead voice. Tim looked at her long slender figure and her neatly rolled straight gold hair in fury and misery. He was always telling his cronies that these cold bitches with *Tatler* backgrounds weren't worth laying – 'their bed manners are so bloody awful,' he used to say amid roars of laughter at the local – but lust and snobbery were too powerful to be resisted in her presence. Even his vanity could not fail to see the bank manager disguised in a uniform which her caricature of him under-lined.

'Very good,' he said laughing. 'I wonder about the moustache though – it's a shade too neat for mine.'

Stephanie looked at him for a second. 'No,' she said, considering, 'I don't think so. I took it from one of those hair-cream advertisements.'

After Tim had gone, Joan Fowler came and fussed round Thea. 'Oh, poor you,' she said, 'it's absolutely monstrous making you take that awful Turnbull on. I hate all these new people. I'm sure we got much more work done when there were only a few of us. Do you remember, Thea, when there was only you and me and Penelope, and then Stephanie came and poor Daphne. Of course, I think it's been *much* worse since Prosser came. A girl in Room 6 told me last night it was simply *frightful* since he'd pushed that creature of his in there. You don't think he'd ever try to do that here, do you? oh, but he *couldn't*, not when you've made so much of Establishments. But then you simply can't tell *what* he might do. If he *did* try to push anyone new in here, I bet you anything nobody would work for them. Even these new girls are frightfully keen on working for you.'

If Joan seized any occasion to surround Thea with a fog of vague perils and implied intrigues, it was not from hostility but from an ill-defined feeling that it united them more closely, made her own protective devotion more necessary – locked in each other's arms for safety they could float for ever upon a buoyant sea of treacly emotion. Unfortunately, however tonic such emotions might be to Joan, Thea only felt their stickiness sucking her down.

Luckily, her experience as guide leader in her father's parish had taught her to keep such silliness in check.

'Don't forget you're chart-checker today, Joan,' she said. 'We keep a half-day chart for every section,' she explained to the new girl. 'Green and red for the two shifts, purple for those on half-days. That's if it's working properly. At the moment Joan's got more than half the section marked on leave.' A little snub worked wonders with these stupid girls, though, really, she had to admit that Joan's devotion was less revolting than the so-called normal attitude that Tim Prosser and the others professed so loudly, a normality that apparently classed human beings with pigs. The nostrils of her bony Roman nose dilated and her thin faintly coloured lips compressed as she thought of it. For a few seconds she imagined the moments of release from it all, and how Colin would be disgusted and amused, and then the horrible realization of Colin's death surged through her head. It was one of those appalling failures of memory that occurred, thank God, increasingly less since his plane had crashed two years before.

Despite the freezing wind that blew across the dismal meadows, where each month saw less trees and more concrete buildings, the atmosphere in the canteen with its radiators and fluorescent lighting was stifling. The white coats of the waitresses were splashed with scraps of food and gravy stains; around their thickly lipsticked mouths, their cheeks and chins shone greasy and sweaty. The youung technician who sat opposite to Thea spat fragments of potato as he talked to his girlfriend. She pushed aside her plate and decided to leave before the roof of her mouth was completely caked in suet. What a prelude to a Mozart concert! she thought. Nothing in her education had ever allowed her to bridge the gap between the material and the cultural.

And yet in some curious way they did get entwined that night. The concert hall was packed when she entered and for a few moments she thought with depression that she would have to stand; of course, with the 'Jupiter' to listen to, she was not likely to mind, but she felt very exhausted. Then suddenly she saw Stephanie's delicate hand beckoning to a seat beside her. How cool and restful her large grey eyes and sleek golden hair seemed above the plain cable-stitch jumper and rope of pearls. Thea felt glad, when she looked round the room at the vulgar evening frocks, that she too had not 'changed'. She was not quite sure that her angora jumper was exactly right, but at any rate her pearls – a twenty-first birthday present from Daddy – were really good. Throughout the Overture to *Figaro* and the 'Jupiter' she had no mind for anything but the music; for she had heard it often enough to be thinking all the time how important it was to know what was coming, otherwise one never really saw the relation of all the parts to each other. The piano concerto that followed was more difficult, and though she tried hard to listen for the themes she found her thoughts wandering.

It was amazing, she reflected, how one person of the right sort could help to make life tolerable. All the vulgarity, the intrigue, the anxiety that surrounded her life at the Bureau seemed to vanish in Stephanie's presence; but that, of course, was because she was so detached, so completely above them. Breeding did make a difference, there was no doubt of it. Not, Thea thought, that she had a reverence for titles in the vulgar, snobbish way that made so many of the girls excited when they saw Stephanie's picture in the *Tatler*. Half of the people in the *Tatler* were appalling, spending their time at night-clubs and theatres, when the country needed them; but the real aristocracy were quite different, living quietly in the country and doing so much good. The proof of it was, of course, that she'd never had one moment's trouble with Stephanie from the day she joined the section. She knew she had a job to do and she did it, which was exactly what one would have expected of course, and she did it so coolly and efficiently too, although

137

she was only twenty, and had beauty that would have turned any other girl's head. With the sound of the piano as an accompaniment, little pictures began to pass before Thea's eyes. She knew Stephanie's home, Garsett House, well from the outside; she used to pass the lodge gates in the bus from Aunt Evelyn's into Taunton, and she had seen the Countess once at a meet of the staghounds near Minehead. Now she saw herself on a horse like Ropey only better, laughing and talking with Stephanie who looked almost haughty in her habit and with her riding whip; or coming down a broad staircase in a plain black evening dress with her pearls, her arm round Stephanie's waist. Stephanie, of course, was in a simple but lovely white frock. Black and white, she pulled herself together as she thought of the advertisement. The slow movement was lovely, but perhaps a little long. It was difficult to imagine the inside of Garsett just from the lodge gates; and Thea felt more safe as she saw Stephanie at the Rectory, galloping on Ropey, for of course, she would not mind his being old and short-winded; or even better, laughing at the strange old hats and frocks in the dressing-up box in the nursery. How pleased Mummy would be with her new friend!

When they came out after the concert Thea almost gasped at the beauty of the moonlight on the snow-covered lawn. After a week's hard frost, the wind was warmer, and already everywhere around them the snow was falling from the branches of the trees with strange, sudden, little popping noises, that relieved the frozen tension. And then, 'How beautiful it is,' Stephanie said, so that Thea almost jumped at the strange unity of their thoughts. They sat waiting in their bus – for their billets were in the same direction – while a crowd of noisy girls from the dance hall climbed into the back seats. Thea, turning round with horror at the sacrilege, saw Turnbull in a dreadful gold lamé evening dress, her bleached streak fallen across her eyes. 'When I say I love you,' she said crooning, 'I want you to know, it isn't because of the moonlight, although 'moonlight becomes you so.' Thea had almost decided to demand silence, when suddenly she saw Stephanie's hair gleam pale golden-green in a haze of moonbeams. Of course, these jazz tunes were very frightful, but in a sense they were the folk music of the age, and she could not help dwelling on the phrase 'moonlight becomes you so', it was strangely like something in a ballad.

'I don't think I can bear tomorrow's party,' said Stephanie suddenly, 'Penelope Rogers has bought a special box of Christmas jokes.' She looked at Thea quizzically, and they both burst out laughing almost hysterically. Stephanie was the first to recover. 'You're tired, Thea,' she said, 'after the way that wretched little man bothered you today. Do you have to come in tomorrow?' and she laid her long fingers on Thea's arm.

'Oh! I think I must,' said Thea, 'but I'm having a quiet Christmas dinner at the billet in the evening.'

'You're lucky,' laughed Stephanie, 'my people have gone away. I shall cook myself an omelette and go to bed.'

'You'll like that, I expect.'

'Oh, I don't know. I'm rather fond of a Christmas celebration as long as it's not at the Bureau.'

'You wouldn't care to come to us, would you?' asked Thea boldly. 'It'll be very quiet, only me and my billetor. She's a dear,' she was about to add that Mrs Owens was a doctor's widow when she wondered if that was exactly the kind of thing that would be of interest to Stephanie, so she said rather pointlessly, 'she's a widow. Do come.'

'Thank you,' said Stephanie, 'I think I should like to,' and then, almost abstractedly, she added, 'You do know, don't you, Thea, what a compensation working for you has been? Compensation for the Bureau being so bloody, I mean.'

It seemed to Thea as though she floated through the gates of the billet – with their brass plate, last remnant of the late Dr Owens – and on up the drive, a cold, white river of moonshine. At any ordinary time she would have recoiled from the melting snow as it seeped through her stockings, for her fastidious feelings revolted from any unfamiliar physical touch, but tonight she was dancing on a lake of glass. No happiness, however, could allow her to forget the consideration due to others, so she removed her shoes most carefully as she closed the front door.

'Thea!' Mrs Owens called from her bedroom upstairs, 'is that you?'

It was a nightly repeated ritual that usually formed the final torture of Thea's tiring and nerve-racked days, but tonight, 'Yes, Mrs Owens. Can I come in for a moment?'

She lay back in the armchair by the old lady's bed and ran her hand sensuously over the soft pink eiderdown, just as she did in the rare, happy, midnight 'confabs' with Mummy, when Daddy was visit-preaching.

'Does anybody in the world make such perfect Ovaltine?' she cried, as she helped herself from the little spirit stove by the bedside. 'Oh, isn't it nice that Christmas is here?' she asked.

'I wish I could do more to make it brighter for you,' said Mrs Owens. 'I think it's a shame they don't send you all home. I've made the sausage rolls for you to take tomorrow. I'm afraid they won't go very far. I nearly let the pastry burn. I've been so excited all day. I've had a letter from Stephen, and he's getting leave in the New Year.'

'Oh! darling!' cried Thea, 'I'm so pleased,' and she leaned over and kissed the old lady.

Mrs Owens was quite surprised by the warmth of her embrace. 'We'll have a real celebration tomorrow evening,' Thea said, 'you must open a bottle of that champagne. Oh, and I've asked someone to come to dinner – Stephanie Reppington.'

'That beautiful girl whose picture was in the *Tatler*? Oh, dear I'm afraid we shan't be grand enough.' It was one of Mrs Owens's constant fears that she would not be able to live up to the social standards of her 'wartime child'.

'Oh Stephanie's not like that,' Thea protested, 'she's tremendously simple and genuine. I know you'll like her.'

'My dear,' said Mrs Owens, 'you know that any friend of yours is welcome here,' and she smiled so sweetly. It was the most wonderful Christmas Eve, just like a fairy story.

By Christmas afternoon the Establishment Room had been quite transformed, and everything was ready for the tea party. Each plywood table was covered with a lace-edged cloth, and right across the centre of the big middle table, where the adding machines usually stood, ran a row of little pots of holly made so cleverly from tinfoil and decorated with little cut-out black cats in bedsocks. A whole collection of 'In' and 'Out' trays had been lined with paper doileys and filled with every sort of delicious cake and sandwich – Thea's sausage rolls and Penelope's dainty bridge rolls filled with sandwich spread, Helen's raspberry fingers and little pyramids of chocolate powder and post toasties that Joan Fowler called 'Coconut Kisses': the extra sugar ration of months had gone into the display. Caricatures of everybody were pinned on the walls, and some drawings of cuties modelled on 'Jane' from the *Daily Mirror*, but less sexy and more whimsical. It had proved very difficult to fit the branches of holly and evergreen to the blue tubular lighting, but by a united effort it had been done; whilst from the central hanging light there swung an enormous and rather menacing bunch of mistletoe. Stephanie had brought six bottles of peaches in brandy from Fortnum's and they stood in uncompromisingly lavish display on the table by the window, until at the last minute Joan Fowler decided to decorate them with crackers and some silver 'stardust' that flew all over the room and stuck to everyone's clothes. At four sharp visitors from other rooms and sections began to arrive.

Never was the dissimilarity, the lack of basic compatibility of the staff of the Bureau more apparent than on such customarily festive occasions as Christmas. Compelled by convention to put aside 'shop' talk and the gossip of personalities which surrounded their working hours, the tightly welded machine parts soon collapsed into a motley collection of totally disparate individuals. The service officers found it impossible to continue to suggest that they were really intellectuals; the businessmen's service talk creaked badly; whilst the assumption of business toughness among the dons and schoolmasters was patently laughable. The women of all ages and classes, who so outnumbered the men at the Bureau, glimpsed with shame something of their failure to preserve the standards of glamour and charm normally offered to the other sex; they saw for a moment that in their fatigue and absorption with routine they had forgotten to turn the males out of the dressing room before it was too late. Everywhere in the room the regulation masks of brightness and competence were slipping, and from behind them peeped forth pre-war faces, pale after so much confinement, and blinking a little at the strange light in which they were seeing the accustomed surroundings, but individual, shy and faintly disgusted with their colleagues. Heaven knows to what anarchy the discipline of years might have slipped, for an hour or more must pass before the circulation of free beer would allow the tough, brassy, devil-take-the-hindmost gang to assume their wonted leadership, but luckily there was another stable, welding element for whom tea and buns was a familiar signal to take control. From Low Church and Chapel, from CICU and OICU, from the hockey field and the football ground – 'God who created me nimble and light of limb' – they were there when needed. All difference, all shyness, was dissolved in the rich strains of 'Holy Night' from manly baritones that were all but tenors, from contraltos in pious hootings, from the sweet sopranos of girls with nice home backgrounds. Unity was for a moment endangered when the girl who ran the Music Club got together with the polo-sweatered organist and tried to raise the artistic tone – it was, after all, the cultural end of England's war service. They just managed to steer through 'All Under the Leaves', but broke down badly on 'Lullay My

142

Liking', when once more the fine old strains with the good old words floated forth, and soon they had sunk from *Oxford Book of Carols* to plain A. and M.

Tim Prosser, like many of the heads, felt rather out of it. But he smiled patronizingly as he always did when things took a religious turn; and even sang feebly once or twice, when old favourites like 'Once in Royal David's City' made an appearance. After a decent interval he turned to his favourite occupation of teasing flirtation. As a result of working with 'highbrows' he had grafted a certain 'clever' undergraduate diction on to his old bank technique with curious results.

'I'm surprised, Pamela,' he said, to his girlfriend – it was part of the ritual always to repeat their Christian names, 'that a fine upstanding example of female emancipation like yourself should wear those outward and visible signs of servitude,' and he gave her earrings a little tug that made her wince.

'Oh, stop it,' she cried, 'you're hurting.'

'Stop it,' he copied her in falsetto, 'does the slave bid her master to cease his attentions? Does Fatima cry to Bluebeard, "hold, enough?" Pamela' – and he looked stern – 'I'm afraid that your visit to London has done you no good.'

'You're the end,' said Pamela.

'The end Pamela, the end. You really must enlarge your vocabulary. Now the middle Pamela, or the beginning, why not try them for a change?'

'Oh stop talking nonsense,' protested the girl.

'I know Pamela, I know. 'Ow I do go on, as the tart said to the sailor. But it's nothing to how I *shall* go on Pamela, if you wrinkle your nose up at me like that. Not that it is different by an inch from any other nose, a hair's breadth shorter perhaps than Cleopatra's, but then you see Pamela, like Mark Antony, I'm funny that way,' and with this he pinched her thigh.

Thea, who was standing near by, tried not to give them

143

the satisfaction of seeing her look the other way. Not that vulgarity could upset her this afternoon. Stephanie had brought her peach offering directly to her and they had stood for a moment side by side. When the singing started, the girl had smiled, 'It's easier really not to believe it's happening,' she had said, and Thea, laughing, had agreed. A few minutes later Stephanie had slipped away, and Thea stood by a window, gazing out on to the wet shiny asphalt paths as though her dreams were reflected in their mirrored surface. She smiled gently at some of her girls from time to time, and, after Stephanie had left, even joined in one of the carols. It was not the sort of singing that would have been favoured at the Rectory – all too hearty and muscular for her father's almost Tractarian taste – so that, happy as she was she could not feel quite 'at home'; she was, therefore, dissociated enough to notice the strained, red face of one of the new conscripts. Clearly the simple emotion of the carols had brought 'home' all too near. Thea's kindly impulses were liberated by her happiness, and, additionally urged by a personal horror of any public scene, she crossed the room, took the girl by the arm and led her out before the pent-up sobbing had attracted much attention.

The empty workrooms, with their litter of papers and tin lids full of cigarette stumps, were not ideal rest rooms, but at last Thea found one with a battered cane armchair. Here she deposited the hysterical girl, provided her with a cigarette and a copy of *Picture Post*, and left her comparatively restored. A faint ray from the dying winter sun shining upon the wet leaves of the laurels tempted Thea to take a turn through the shrubbery.

She had never been a light-hearted girl, had always walked a tightrope across chasms of social anxiety and private phobia, and, since Colin's death, she had been ceaselessly battling to keep within her strict limits of propriety the violent anger and frustration into which it had plunged her. Now, therefore, that this sudden release from isolation had come, she was constrained by habit to savour it in quietude rather than to laugh and sing out loud as her excited senses urged. She sat on the garden seat under the high cypress hedge that cut the shrubbery in two, and gave herself up to hazy pictures of the future, as she had not dared to do for over two years. She had just been dissuaded by Stephanie's good sense from foolish investment of the proceeds of the little hat shop they had both been so successfully running for some years in Brook Street, when she heard voices approaching from the other side of the cypress hedge. It was the sound of her own name – how often had her self-consciousness imagined this over the last years, but this time she was not mistaken – that recalled her from her dreams.

'I simply don't understand all this Thea business,' a man's voice was saying; she recognized him as one of the boys from the Archives Section – Noah's Ark Cubs they were always called by the others, 'but do exactly what you like.'

And then it was Stephanie's voice that replied, 'But naturally, Nigel, you know that I always do.'

Thea stood up so that they should see her before more could be said; it was one of the primary rules of conduct that her mother had instilled into her. Stephanie's lips parted for a second in surprise, then, 'Oh, Thea,' she said, 'I was coming to look for you. Nigel's asked us to go to their section dance. I said I had no idea what you'd arranged . . .'

'But, of course, you must go,' cried Thea, she felt sure that her lips looked blue with the cold.

'But is it what *you* would like, darling?' asked Stephanie.

'Oh, *I* shouldn't be able to go, I'm afraid, you see I told Mrs Owens . . .' Thea seemed to remember vaguely that this whole conversation had taken place many times before, could anticipate the disappointment and anger that burnt her as though it was a scene she had been rehearsing all her life.

'Oh, well, of course we can't come then, Nigel,' Stephanie

said hurriedly, and when the young man murmured something about promises, she added sharply, 'Don't be absurd, Nigel, you know I never make promises.'

'Please, Stephanie,' said Thea, 'I'm sure you'd enjoy it much more. It'll only be a Christmas dinner at the billet, I'm afraid it'll be very boring.'

Stephanie raised her eyebrows slightly and her voice was faintly disgusted, as she answered, 'My dear, as if everything here wasn't boring. See you tomorrow, Nigel,' she added in dismissal. She was clearly anxious that he should not witness Thea's emotion further. They stood for a moment silent after Nigel had gone.

'You *would* have liked to have gone . . .' began Thea, when Stephanie interrupted quite angrily, 'Good heavens, I'm perfectly indifferent what I do,' she cried; a moment later, she laughed rather shrilly, 'I'm sorry,' she said, 'I'm afraid I'm not very good at all this. You see, it never occurs to me to think of anything that happens here as being important,' and she disappeared into the house.

After a little Thea crept back to the shadow of the building. She stood for a moment, leaning against the brick wall, deliberately feeling its harsh surface through her costume, controlling a violent impulse to run after Stephanie and beg her asssurance that the whole conversation had been an illusion, had never taken place, had been a joke . . . Then, carefully shaping her mouth with lipstick, she returned to the party.

Already beer drinking had begun and the carol singers were giving way to Tim and the 'gang'. A gramophone was playing 'Paper Doll', 'I'd rather have a paper doll to call my own' the crooner sang 'than a fickle-minded real live girl.' Thea accepted a strong gin, coughed at the first mouthful, and then with set expression, joined the little group surrounding Tim and his girlfriend.

'Cry-baby all right now?' the girlfriend asked, and 'Yes,' answered Thea. 'cry-baby's all right.'

'My God! I don't know what they expect,' said Tim.

'No,' replied Thea, 'you don't, Tim, you don't know what they expect.'

'So that's for you, Tim,' said one of the group.

'Oh, Thea and I understand each other, don't we Thea?' said Tim, and, 'Oh yes, we understand each other, Tim,' Thea said. She felt sure this was the right manner – bitter, quick, hard – it brought back something she had read in Hemingway, and the loud noise of the gramophone seemed to clinch the scene. In reality she didn't feel at all bitter, only humiliated and unhappy.

'Well,' said Tim, 'here's to next Christmas, and the one after!'

'Think we'll be here, Tim?' asked a young lieutenant.

'Shouldn't be surprised,' said Tim, 'got 'em on the run now, you know, and we've got to paste the bastards until they've forgotten *how* to squeal. Besides there's always the Nips.' Two drinks always made him talk in this saloon-bar manner, unless one of his superiors was about, when he tried to preserve some of his hard-won gentlemanly behaviour.

'Two years from now, you'll be Deputy Director, Tim, and won't that be nice,' Thea said. She had taken another drink and was prepared to say anything if only they would like her.

'She's got you there, Tim,' they cried, and Tim said, 'Touché. But honestly, Thea, you know as well as I do we can't let up now,' he looked serious.

Thea, too, looked grave. 'I know, Tim,' she said simply, though she wasn't quite sure to what he referred.

'Well, when you two have settled all our fates,' said the girlfriend, 'we've got to move, darling.'

Thea was amused to see that the girl was slightly jealous, so she smiled at Tim quizzically. Strangely enough he didn't respond, but followed his girlfriend. Thea was puzzled, her memory of scenes on the films had been different from this.

Suddenly everyone moved off, and Thea found herself isolated again. She felt so unhappy that she could hardly restrain her tears. She had worked up a special vulgar manner, and there she was left with it on her hands. Suddenly she saw Stephanie coming towards her, and desperately she made for where Joan Fowler stood.

'Oh! Joan, we ought to be going,' she cried. 'I told my billet eight o'clock sharp and I've ordered a special car.'

Joan Fowler looked bemused, but in a mist of happiness.

'Oh! Thea, I didn't remember. I *did* say to Penelope . . . oh! but it'll be quite all right. Shall I get my coat?' she cried.

Thea turned to Stephanie. 'Oh my dear,' she said, drawling, 'it's too awful of me. I quite forgot last night, when I asked you, that Joan was coming. I was half asleep, I think. I'm afraid I daren't spring an unexpected guest on poor Mrs Owens, ours is such a *very* humble home. But you won't have missed anything, I'm sure you'd have found it an *awful* bore.'

ROBERT LOUIS STEVENSON

'Vailima'

To S. R. Crockett
On receiving a Dedication

Blows the wind today, and the sun and the rain are flying,
   Blows the wind on the moors today and now,
Where about the graves of the martyrs the whaups are
     crying,
   My heart remembers how!

Grey recumbent tombs of the dead in desert places,
   Standing stones on the vacant wine-red moor,
Hills of sheep, and the howes of the silent vanished races,
   And winds, austere and pure.

Be it granted to me to behold you again in dying,
   Hills of home! and to hear again the call;
Hear about the graves of the martyrs the peewees crying,
   And hear no more at all.

CHARLOTTE BRONTË

from *Jane Eyre*

Meantime, Mr Brocklehurst, standing on the hearth with his hands behind his back, majestically surveyed the whole school. Suddenly his eye gave a blink, as if it had met something that either dazzled or shocked its pupil; turning, he said in more rapid accents than he had hitherto used, 'Miss Temple, Miss Temple, what – *what* is that girl with curled hair? Red hair, ma'am, curled – curled all over?' And extending his cane he pointed to the awful object, his hand shaking as he did so.

'It is Julia Severn,' replied Miss Temple, very quietly.

'Julia Severn, ma'am! And why has she, or any other, curled hair? Why, in defiance of every precept and principle of this house, does she conform to the world so openly – here in an evangelical, charitable establishment – as to wear her hair one mass of curls?'

'Julia's hair curls naturally,' returned Miss Temple, still more quietly.

'Naturally! Yes, but we are not to conform to nature: I wish these girls to be the children of Grace: and why that abundance? I have again and again intimated that I desire the hair to be arranged closely, modestly, plainly. Miss Temple, that girl's hair must be cut off entirely; I will send a barber to-morrow: and I see others who have far too much of the excrescence – that tall girl, tell her to turn round. Tell all the first form to rise up and direct their faces to the wall.'

Miss Temple passed the handkerchief over her lips, as if to smooth away the involuntary smile that curled them; she gave the order, however, and when the first class could take in what was required of them, they obeyed. Leaning a little back on my bench, I could see the looks and grimaces with which they commented on this manoeuvre: it was a pity Mr Brocklehurst could not see them too; he would perhaps have felt that, whatever he might do with the outside of the cup and platter, inside was further beyond his interference than he imagined.

He scrutinized the reverse of these living medals some five minutes, then pronounced sentence. These words fell like the knell of doom: 'All these top-knots must be cut off.'

Miss Temple seemed to remonstrate.

'Madam,' he pursued, 'I have a Master to serve whose kingdom is not of this world: my mission is to mortify in these girls the lusts of the flesh; to teach them to clothe themselves with shame-facedness and sobriety, not with braided hair and costly apparel; and each of the young persons before us has a string of hair twisted in plaits which vanity itself might have woven: these, I repeat, must be cut off; think of the time wasted, of—'

Mr Brocklehurst was here interrupted: three other visitors, ladies, now entered the room. They ought to have come a little sooner to have heard his lecture on dress, for they were splendidly attired in velvet, silk and furs. The two younger of the trio (fine girls of sixteen and seventeen) had grey beaver hats, then in fashion, shaded with ostrich plumes, and from under the brim of this graceful headdress fell a profusion of light tresses, elaborately curled; the elderly lady was enveloped in a costly velvet shawl, trimmed with ermine, and she wore a false front of French curls.

These ladies were deferentially received by Miss Temple, as Mrs and Misses Brocklehurst, and conducted to seats of honour at the top of the room. It seems they had come in the carriage with their reverend relative, and had been conducting a rummaging scrutiny of the rooms upstairs, while he transacted business with the housekeeper, questioned the laundress and lectured the superintendent. They now proceeded to address divers remarks and reproofs to Miss Smith, who was charged with the care of the linen and the inspection of the dormitories: but I had no time to listen to what they said; other matters called off and enchained my attention.

Hitherto, while gathering up the discourse of Mr Brocklehurst and Miss Temple, I had not, at the same time, neglected precautions to secure my personal safety; which I thought would be effected, if I could only elude observation. To this end, I had sat well back on the form, and while seeming to be busy with my sum, had held my slate in such a manner as to conceal my face: I might have escaped notice, had not my treacherous slate somehow happened to slip from my hand, and falling with an obtrusive crash, directly drawn every eye upon me; I knew it was all over now, and, as I stooped to pick up the two fragments of slate, I rallied my forces for the worst. It came.

'A careless girl!' said Mr Brocklehurst, and immediately after, 'It is the new pupil, I perceive.' And before I could draw breath, 'I must not forget I have a word to say respecting her.' Then aloud: how loud it seemed to me! 'Let the child who broke her slate, come forward!'

Of my own accord, I could not have stirred; I was paralysed: but the two great girls who sat on each side of me, set me on my legs and pushed me towards the dread judge, and then Miss Temple gently assisted me to his very feet, and I caught her whispered counsel.

'Don't be afraid, Jane, I saw it was an accident; you shall not be punished.'

The kind whisper went to my heart like a dagger.

'Another minute, and she will despise me for a hypocrite,' thought I; and an impulse of fury against Reed, Brocklehurst and Co. bounded in my pulses at the conviction. I was no Helen Burns.

'Fetch that stool,' said Mr Brocklehurst, pointing to a very high one from which a monitor had just risen: it was brought.

'Place the child upon it.'

And I was placed there, by whom I don't know: I was in no condition to note particulars; I was only aware that they had hoisted me up to the height of Mr Brocklehurst's nose, that he was within a yard of me, and that a spread of shot orange and purple silk pelisses, and a cloud of silvery plumage extended and waved below me.

Mr Brocklehurst hemmed. 'Ladies,' said he, turning to his family: 'Miss Temple, teachers, and children, you all see this girl?'

Of course they did; for I felt their eyes directed like burning-glasses against my scorched skin.

'You see she is yet young; you observe she possesses the ordinary form of childhood; God has graciously given her the shape that He has given to all of us; no signal deformity points her out as a marked character. Who would think that the Evil One had already found a servant and agent in her? Yet such, I grieve to say, is the case.'

A pause – in which I began to steady the palsy of my nerves, and to feel that the Rubicon was passed; and that the trial, no longer to be shirked, must be firmly sustained.

'My dear children,' pursued the black marble clergyman, with pathos, 'this is a sad, a melancholy occasion; for it becomes my duty to warn you, that this girl, who might be one of God's own lambs, is a little castaway: not a member of the true flock, but evidently an interloper and an alien. You must be on your guard against her; you must shun her example: if necessary, avoid her company, exclude her from your sports, and shut her out from your converse. Teachers, you must watch her: keep your eyes on her movements, weigh well her words, scrutinize her actions, punish her body to save her soul: if, indeed, such salvation be possible, for (my tongue falters while I tell it) this girl, this child, the native of a Christian land, worse than many a little heathen who says its prayers to Brahma and kneels before Juggernaut – this girl is – a liar!'

Now came a pause of ten minutes; during which I, by this time in perfect possession of my wits, observed all the female Brocklehursts produce their pocket-handkerchiefs and apply them to their optics, while the elderly lady swayed herself to and fro, and the two younger ones whispered, 'How shocking!'

Mr Brocklehurst resumed. 'This I learned from her benefactress; from the pious and charitable lady who adopted her in her orphan state, reared her as her own daughter, and whose kindness, whose generosity the unhappy girl repaid by an ingratitude so bad, so dreadful, that at last her excellent patroness was obliged to separate her from her own young ones, fearful lest her vicious example should contaminate their purity: she has sent her here to be healed, even as the Jews of old sent their diseased to the troubled pool of Bethesda; and, teachers, superintendent, I beg of you not to allow the waters to stagnate round her.'

With this sublime conclusion, Mr Brocklehurst adjusted the top button of his surtout, muttered something to his family, who rose, bowed to Miss Temple, and then all the great people sailed in state from the room.

Turning at the door, my judge said, 'Let her stand half an hour longer on that stool, and let no one speak to her during the remainder of the day.'

There was I, then, mounted aloft; I who had said I could not bear the shame of standing on my natural feet in the middle of the room, was now exposed to general view on a pedestal of infamy. What my sensations were, no language can describe; but just as they all rose, stifling my breath and constricting my throat, a girl came up and passed me: in passing, she lifted her eyes. What a strange light inspired them! What an extraordinary sensation that ray sent through me! How the new feeling bore me up! It was as if a martyr, a hero, had passed a slave or victim, and imparted strength in the transit. I mastered the rising hysteria, lifted up my head, and took a firm stand on the stool. Helen Burns asked some slight question about her work of Miss Smith, was chidden for the triviality of the inquiry, returned to her place and smiled at me as she again went by. What a smile! I remember it now, and I know that it was the effluence of fine intellect, of true courage; it lit up her marked lineaments, her thin face, her sunken grey eye, like a reflection from the aspect of an angel. Yet at that moment Helen Burns wore on her arm 'the untidy badge'; scarcely an hour ago I had heard her condemned by Miss Scatcherd to a dinner of bread and water on the morrow, because she had blotted an exercise in copying it out. Such is the imperfect nature of man! Such spots are there on the disc of the clearest planet; and eyes like Miss Scatcherd's can only see those minute defects, and are blind to the full brightness of the orb.

Ere the half-hour ended, five o'clock struck; school was dismissed, and all were gone into the refectory to tea. I now ventured to descend: it was deep dusk; I retired into a corner and sat down on the floor. The spell by which I had been so far supported began to dissolve; reaction took place, and soon, so overwhelming was the grief that seized me, I sank prostrate with my face to the ground. Now I wept: Helen Burns was not here; nothing sustained me; left to myself I abandoned myself, and my tears watered the boards. I had meant to be so good, and to do so much at Lowood: to make so many friends, to earn respect and win affection. Already I had made visible progress: that very morning I had reached the head of my class; Miss Miller had praised me warmly; Miss Temple had smiled approbation; she had promised to teach me drawing, and to let me learn French, if I continued to make similar improvement two months longer: and then I was well received by my fellow-pupils; treated as an equal by those of my own age, and not molested by any; now, here I lay again crushed and trodden on; and could I ever rise more?

'Never,' I thought; and ardently I wished to die. While sobbing out this wish in broken accents, someone approached: I started up – again Helen Burns was near me; the fading fires just showed her coming up the long, vacant room; she brought my coffee and bread.

'Come, eat something,' she said; but I put both away from me, feeling as if a drop or a crumb would have choked me in my present condition. Helen regarded me, probably with surprise: I could not now abate my agitation, though I tried hard; I continued to weep aloud. She sat down on the ground near me, embraced her knees with her arms and rested her head upon them; in that attitude she remained silent as an Indian. I was the first who spoke.

'Helen, why do you stay with a girl whom everybody believes to be a liar?'

'Everybody, Jane? Why, there are only eighty people who have heard you called so, and the world contains hundreds of millions.'

'But what have I to do with millions? The eighty I know despise me.'

'Jane, you are mistaken: probably not one in the school either despises or dislikes you: many, I am sure, pity you much.'

'How can they pity me after what Mr Brocklehurst said?'

'Mr Brocklehurst is not a god: nor is he even a great and admired man; he is little liked here; he never took steps to make himself liked. Had he treated you as an especial favourite, you would have found enemies, declared or covert, all around you; as it is, the greater number would offer you sympathy if they dared. Teachers and pupils may look coldly on you for a day or two, but friendly feelings are concealed in their hearts; and if you persevere in doing well, these feelings will ere long appear so much the more evidently for their temporary suppression. Besides, Jane,' – she paused.

'Well, Helen?' said I, putting my hand into hers: she chafed my fingers gently to warm them, and went on.

'If all the world hated you, and believed you wicked, while your own conscience approved you, and absolved you from guilt, you would not be without friends.'

'No; I know I should think well of myself; but that is not enough: if others don't love me, I would rather die than live – I cannot bear to be solitary and hated, Helen. Look here; to gain some real affection from you, or Miss Temple, or any other whom I truly love, I would willingly submit to have the bone of my arm broken, or to let a bull toss me, or to stand behind a kicking horse, and let it dash its hoof at my chest—'

'Hush, Jane! you think too much of the love of human beings: you are too impulsive, too vehement: the sovereign hand that created your frame, and put life into it, has provided you with other resources than your feeble self, or than creatures feeble as you. Besides this earth, and besides the race of men, there is an invisible world and a kingdom of spirits: that world is round us, for it is everywhere; and those spirits watch us, for they are commissioned to guard us; and if we were dying in pain and shame, if scorn smote us on all sides, and hatred crushed us, angels see our tortures, recognize our innocence (if innocent we be: as I know you are of this charge which Mr Brocklehurst has weakly and pompously repeated at second-hand from Mrs Reed; for I read a sincere nature in your ardent eyes and on your clear front), and God waits only the separation of spirit from flesh to crown us with a full reward. Why, then, should we ever sink overwhelmed with distress, when life is so soon over, and death is so certain an entrance to happiness – to glory?'

I was silent: Helen had calmed me; but in the tranquillity she imparted there was an alloy of inexpressible sadness. I felt the impression of woe as she spoke, but I could not tell whence it came; and when, having done speaking, she breathed a little fast and coughed a short cough, I momentarily forgot my own sorrows to yield to a vague concern for her.

Resting my head on Helen's shoulder, I put my arms round her waist; she drew me to her, and we reposed in silence. We had not sat long thus, when another person came in. Some heavy clouds, swept from the sky by a rising wind, had left the moon bare; and her light, streaming in through a window near, shone full both on us and on the approaching figure, which we at once recognized as Miss Temple.

'I came on purpose to find you, Jane Eyre,' said she; 'I want you in my room; and as Helen Burns is with you, she may come too.'

We went; following the superintendent's guidance, we had to thread some intricate passages, and mount a staircase before we reached her apartment; it contained a good fire, and looked cheerful. Miss Temple told Helen Burns to be seated in a low armchair on one side of the hearth, and herself taking another, she called me to her side.

'Is it all over?' she asked, looking down at my face. 'Have you cried your grief away?'

'I am afraid I never shall do that.'

'Why?'

'Because I have been wrongly accused; and you, ma'am, and everybody else will now think me wicked.'

'We shall think you what you prove yourself to be, my child. Continue to act as a good girl, and you will satisfy me.'

'Shall I, Miss Temple?'

'You will,' said she, passing her arm round me. 'And now tell me who is the lady whom Mr Brocklehurst called your benefactress?'

'Mrs Reed, my uncle's wife. My uncle is dead, and he left me to her care.'

'Did she not, then, adopt you of her own accord?'

'No, ma'am; she was sorry to have to do it: but my uncle, as I have often heard the servants say, got her to promise before he died, that she would always keep me.'

'Well now, Jane, you know, or at least I will tell you, that when a criminal is accused, he is always allowed to speak in his own defence. You have been charged with falsehood; defend yourself to me as well as you can. Say whatever your memory suggests as true; but add nothing and exaggerate nothing.'

I resolved, in the depth of my heart, that I would be most moderate – most correct; and, having reflected a few minutes in order to arrange coherently what I had to say, I told her all the story of my sad childhood. Exhausted by emotion, my language was more subdued than it generally was when it developed that sad theme; and mindful of Helen's warnings against the indulgence of resentment, I infused into the narrative far less of gall and wormwood than ordinary. Thus restrained and simplified, it sounded more credible: I felt as I went on that Miss Temple fully believed me.

In the course of the tale I had mentioned Mr Lloyd as having come to see me after the fit: for I never forgot the, to me, frightful episode of the red room; in detailing which, my excitement was sure, in some degree, to break bounds; for nothing could soften in my recollection the spasm of agony which clutched my heart when Mrs Reed spurned my wild supplication for pardon, and locked me a second time in the dark and haunted chamber.

I had finished: Miss Temple regarded me a few minutes in silence; she then said, 'I know something of Mr Lloyd; I shall write to him; if his reply agrees with your statement, you shall be publicly cleared from every imputation: to me, Jane, you are clear now.'

She kissed me, and still keeping me at her side (where I was well contented to stand, for I derived a child's pleasure from the contemplation of her face, her dress, her one or two ornaments, her white forehead, her clustered and shining curls, and beaming dark eyes), she proceeded to address Helen Burns.

'How are you tonight, Helen? Have you coughed much today?'

'Not quite so much I think, ma'am.'

'And the pain in your chest?'

'It is a little better.'

Miss Temple got up, took her hand and examined her pulse; then she returned to her own seat: as she resumed it, I heard her sigh low. She was pensive a few minutes, then rousing herself, she said cheerfully, 'But you two are my visitors tonight; I must treat you as such.' She rang the bell.

'Barbara,' she said to the servant who answered it, 'I have not yet had tea; bring the tray, and place cups for these two young ladies.'

And a tray was soon brought. How pretty, to my eyes, did the china and bright teapot look, placed on the little round table near the fire! How fragrant was the steam of the beverage and the scent of the toast! Of which, however, I, to my dismay (for I was beginning to be hungry), discerned only a very small portion: Miss Temple discerned it too.

'Barbara,' said she, 'can you not bring a little more bread and butter? There is not enough for three.'

Barbara went out: she returned soon.

'Madam, Mrs Harden says she has sent up the usual quantity.'

Mrs Harden, be it observed, was the housekeeper: a woman after Mr Brocklehurst's own heart, made up of equal parts of whalebone and iron.

'Oh, very well!' returned Miss Temple; 'we must make it do, Barbara, I suppose.' And as the girl withdrew, she added, smiling, 'Fortunately, I have it in my power to supply deficiencies for this once.'

Having invited Helen and me to approach the table, and placed before each of us a cup of tea with one delicious but thin morsel of toast, she got up, unlocked a drawer, and taking from it a parcel wrapped in paper, disclosed presently to our eyes a good-sized seed-cake.

'I meant to give each of you some of this to take with you,' said she; 'but as there is so little toast, you must have it now,' and she proceeded to cut slices with a generous hand.

We feasted that evening as on nectar and ambrosia; and not the light delight of the entertainment was the smile of gratification with which our hostess regarded us, as we satisfied our famished appetites on the delicate fare she liberally supplied. Tea over and the tray removed, she again summoned us to the fire; we sat one on each side of her, and now a conversation followed between her and Helen, which it was indeed a privilege to be admitted to hear.

Miss Temple had always something of serenity in her air, of state in her mien, of refined propriety in her language, which precluded deviation into the ardent, the excited, the eager: something which chastened the pleasure of those who looked on her and listened to her, by a controlling sense of awe; and such was my feeling now: but as to Helen Burns, I was struck with wonder.

The refreshing meal, the brilliant fire, the presence and kindness of her beloved instructress, or, perhaps, more than all these, something in her own unique mind, had roused her powers within her. They woke, they kindled: first, they glowed in the bright tint of her cheek, which till this hour I had never seen but pale and bloodless; then they shone in the liquid lustre of her eyes, which had suddenly acquired a beauty more singular than that of Miss Temple's – a beauty neither of fine colour nor long eyelash, nor pencilled brow, but of meaning, of movement, of radiance. Then her soul sat on her lips, and language flowed, from what source I cannot tell: has a girl of fourteen a heart large enough, vigorous enough to hold the swelling spring of pure, full, fervid eloquence? Such was the characteristic of Helen's discourse on that, to me, memorable evening; her spirit seemed hastening to live within a very brief span as much as many live during a protracted existence.

They conversed of things I had never heard of; of nations and times past; of countries far away; of secrets of nature discovered or guessed at: they spoke of books: how many they had read! What stores of knowledge they possessed! Then they seemed so familiar with French names and

French authors: but my amazement reached its climax when Miss Temple asked Helen if she sometimes snatched a moment to recall the Latin her father had taught her, and taking a book from a shelf, bade her read and construe a page of Virgil; and Helen obeyed, my organ of veneration expanding at every sounding line. She had scarcely finished ere the bell announced bedtime: no delay could be admitted; Miss Temple embraced us both, saying, as she drew us to her heart, 'God bless you, my children!'

Helen she held a little longer than me: she let her go more reluctantly; it was Helen her eye followed to the door; it was for her she a second time breathed a sad sigh; for her she wiped a tear from her cheek.

On reaching the bedroom, we heard the voice of Miss Scatcherd: she was examining drawers; she had just pulled out Helen Burns's, and when we entered Helen was greeted with a sharp reprimand, and told that tomorrow she should have half a dozen of untidily folded articles pinned to her shoulder.

'My things were indeed in shameful disorder,' murmured Helen to me, in a low voice: 'I intended to have arranged them, but I forgot.'

Next morning, Miss Scatcherd wrote in conspicuous characters on a piece of pasteboard the word 'slattern', and bound it like a phylactery round Helen's large, mild, intelligent and benign-looking forehead. She wore it till evening, patient, unresentful, regarding it as a deserved punishment. The moment Miss Scatcherd withdrew after afternoon school, I ran to Helen, tore it off, and thrust it into the fire: the fury of which she was incapable had been burning in my soul all day, and tears, hot and large, had continually been scalding my cheek; for the spectacle of her sad resignation gave me an intolerable pain at the heart.

About a week subsequently to the incidents above narrated, Miss Temple, who had written to Mr Lloyd, received his answer: it appeared that what he said went to corroborate my account. Miss Temple, having assembled the whole school, announced that inquiry had been made into the charges alleged against Jane Eyre, and that she was most happy to be able to pronounce her completely cleared from every imputation. The teachers then shook hands with me and kissed me, and a murmur of pleasure ran through the ranks of my companions.

Thus relieved of a grievous load, I from that hour set to work afresh, resolved to pioneer my way through every difficulty: I toiled hard, and my success was proportionate to my efforts; my memory, not naturally tenacious, improved with practice; exercise sharpened my wits; in a few weeks I was promoted to a higher class; in less than two months I was allowed to commence French and drawing. I learned the first two tenses of the verb *être*, and sketched my first cottage (whose walls, by-the-by, outrivalled in slope those of the leaning tower of Pisa), on the same day. That night, on going to bed, I forgot to prepare in imagination the Barmecide supper of hot roast potatoes, or white bread and new milk, with which I was wont to amuse my inward cravings: I feasted instead on the spectacle of ideal drawings, which I saw in the dark; all the work of my own hands: freely pencilled houses and trees, picturesque rocks and ruins, Cuyp-like groups of cattle, sweet paintings of butterflies hovering over unblown roses, of birds picking at ripe cherries, of wrens' nests enclosing pearl-like eggs, wreathed about with young ivy sprays. I examined, too, in thought, the possibility of my ever being able to translate currently a certain little French storybook which Madame Pierrot had that day shown me; nor was that problem solved to my satisfaction ere I fell sweetly asleep.

Well has Solomon said – 'Better is a dinner of herbs where love is, than a stalled ox and hatred therewith.'

I would not now have exchanged Lowood with all its privations, for Gateshead and its daily luxuries.

But the privations, or rather the hardships, of Lowood lessened. Spring drew on, she was indeed already come; the frosts of winter had ceased; its snows were melted, its cutting winds ameliorated. My wretched feet, flayed and swollen to lameness by the sharp air of January, began to heal and subside under the gentler breathings of April; the nights and mornings no longer by their Canadian temperature froze the very blood in our veins; we could now endure the play-hour in the garden: sometimes on a sunny day it began even to be pleasant and genial, and a greenness grew over those brown beds, which, freshening daily, suggested the thought that Hope traversed them at night, and left each morning brighter traces of her steps. Flowers peeped out amongst the leaves; snowdrops, crocuses, purple auriculas and golden-eyed pansies. On Thursday afternoons (half-holidays) we now took walks, and found still sweeter flowers opening by the wayside, under the hedges.

I discovered, too, that a great pleasure, an enjoyment which the horizon only bounded, lay all outside the high and spike-guarded walls of our garden: this pleasure consisted in prospect of noble summits girdling a great hill-hollow, rich in verdure and shadow: in a bright beck, full of dark stones and sparkling eddies. How different had this scene looked when I viewed it laid out beneath the iron sky of winter, stiffened in frost, shrouded with snow – when mists as chill as death wandered to the impulse of east winds along those purple peaks, and rolled down 'ing' and holm till they blended with the frozen fog of the beck! That beck itself was then a torrent, turbid and curbless: it tore asunder the wood, and sent a raving sound through the air, often thickened with wild rain or whirling sleet; and for the forest on its banks, *that* showed only ranks of skeletons.

April advanced to May: a bright, serene May it was; days of blue sky, placid sunshine, and soft western or southern gales filled up its duration. And now vegetation matured with vigour; Lowood shook loose its tresses; it became all green, all flowery; its great elm, ash, and oak skeletons were restored to majestic life; woodland plants sprang up profusely in its recesses; unnumbered varieties of moss filled its hollows, and it made a strange ground-sunshine out of the wealth of its wild primrose plants: I have seen their pale gold gleam in overshadowed spots like scatterings of the sweetest lustre. All this I enjoyed often and fully, free, unwatched, and almost alone; for this unwonted liberty and pleasure there was a cause, to which it now becomes my task to advert.

Have I not described a pleasant site for a dwelling, when I speak of it as bosomed in hill and wood, and rising from the verge of a stream? Assuredly, pleasant enough: but whether healthy or not is another question.

That forest-dell, where Lowood lay, was the cradle of fog and fog-bred pestilence; which, quickening with the quickening spring, crept into the Orphan Asylum, breathed typhus through its crowded schoolroom and dormitory, and, ere May arrived, transformed the seminary into a hospital.

Semi-starvation and neglected colds had predisposed most of the pupils to receive infection: forty-five out of the eighty girls lay ill at one time. Classes were broken up, rules relaxed. The few who continued well were allowed almost unlimited licence; because the medical attendant insisted on the necessity of frequent exercise to keep them in health: and had it been otherwise, no one had leisure to watch or restrain them. Miss Temple's whole attention was absorbed by the patients: she lived in the sickroom, never quitting it except to snatch a few hours' rest at night. The teachers were fully occupied with packing up and making other necessary preparations for the departure of those girls who were fortunate enough to have friends and relations able and willing to remove them from the seat of contagion. Many, already smitten, went home only to die; some died at the school, and were buried quietly and quickly, the nature of the malady forbidding delay.

While disease had thus become an inhabitant of Lowood, and death its frequent visitor; while there was gloom and fear within its walls; while its rooms and passages steamed with hospital smells, the drug and the pastille striving vainly to overcome the effluvia of mortality, that bright May shone unclouded over the bold hills and beautiful woodland out of doors. Its garden, too, glowed with flowers: hollyhocks had sprung up tall as trees, lilies had opened, tulips and roses were in bloom; the borders of the little beds were gay with pink thrift and crimson double daisies; the sweet briars gave out, morning and evening, their scent of spice and apples; and these fragrant treasures were all useless for most of the inmates of Lowood, except to furnish now and then a handful of herbs and blossoms to put in a coffin.

But I, and the rest who continued well, enjoyed fully the beauties of the scene and season: they let us ramble in the wood, like gipsies, from morning till night; we did what we liked, went where we liked: we lived better too. Mr Brocklehurst and his family never came near Lowood now: household matters were not scrutinized into: the cross housekeeper was gone, driven away by the fear of infection; her successor, who had been matron at the Lowton Dispensary, unused to the ways of her new abode, provided with comparative liberality. Besides, there were fewer to feed: the sick could eat little; our breakfast basins were better filled: when there was no time to prepare a regular dinner, which often happened, she would give us a large piece of cold pie, or a thick slice of bread and cheese, and this we carried away with us to the wood, where we each chose the spot we liked best, and dined sumptuously.

My favourite seat was a smooth and broad stone, rising white and dry from the very middle of the beck, and only to be got at by wading through the water; a feat I accomplished barefoot. The stone was just broad enough to accommodate, comfortably, another girl and me, at that time my chosen comrade – one Mary Ann Wilson; a shrewd observant personage, whose society I took pleasure in, partly because she was witty and original, and partly because she had a manner which set me at my ease. Some years older than I, she knew more of the world, and could tell me many things I liked to hear; with her my curiosity found gratification; to my faults also she gave ample indulgence, never imposing curb or rein on anything I said. She had a turn for narrative, I for analysis; she liked to inform, I to question; so we got on swimmingly together, deriving much entertainment, if not much improvement, from our mutual intercourse.

And where, meantime, was Helen Burns? Why did I not spend these sweet days of liberty with her? Had I forgotten her? Or was I so worthless as to have grown tired of her pure society? Surely the Mary Ann Wilson I have mentioned was inferior to my first acquaintance: she could only tell me amusing stories, and reciprocate any racy and pungent gossip I chose to indulge in; while, if I have spoken truth of Helen, she was qualified to give those who enjoyed the privilege of her converse, a taste of far higher things.

True, reader; and I knew and felt this: and though I am a defective being, with many faults and few redeeming points, yet I never tired of Helen Burns; nor ever ceased to cherish for her a sentiment of attachment, as strong, tender and respectful as any that ever animated my heart. How could it be otherwise, when Helen, at all times and under all circumstances, evinced for me a quiet and faithful friendship, which ill-humour never soured, nor irritation ever troubled? But Helen was ill at present: for some weeks she had been removed from my sight to I knew not what room upstairs. She was not, I was told, in the hospital portion of the house with the fever patients; for her complaint was consumption, not typhus: and by consumption I, in my ignorance, understood something mild, which time and care would be sure to alleviate.

I was confirmed in this idea by the fact of her once or twice coming downstairs on very warm sunny afternoons, and being taken by Miss Temple into the garden: but, on these occasions, I was not allowed to go and speak to her; I only saw her from the schoolroom window, and then not distinctly; for she was much wrapped up, and sat at a distance under the verandah.

One evening, in the beginning of June, I had stayed out very late with Mary Ann in the wood; we had, as usual, separated ourselves from the others, and had wandered far: so far that we lost our way, and had to ask it at a lonely cottage, where a man and woman lived, who looked after a herd of half-wild swine that fed on the mast in the wood. When we got back, it was after moonrise: a pony, which we knew to be the surgeon's, was standing at the garden door. Mary Ann remarked that she supposed some one must be very ill, as Mr Bates had been sent for at that time of the evening. She went into the house; I stayed behind a few minutes to plant in my garden a handful of roots I had dug up in the forest, and which I feared would wither if I left them till the morning. This done, I lingered yet a little longer: the flowers smelt so sweet as the dew fell; it was such a pleasant evening, so serene, so warm; the still glowing west promised so fairly another fine day on the morrow; the moon rose with such majesty in the grave east. I was noting these things and enjoying them as a child might, when it entered my mind as it had never done before, 'How sad to be lying now on a sick bed, and to be in danger of dying! This world is pleasant – it would be dreary to be called from it, and to have to go who knows where?'

And then my mind made its first earnest effort to comprehend what had been infused into it concerning heaven and hell: and for the first time it recoiled, baffled; and for the first time glancing behind, on each side, and before it, it saw all round an unfathomed gulf: it felt the one point where it stood – the present; all the rest was formless cloud and vacant depth: and it shuddered at the thought of tottering, and plunging amid that chaos. While pondering this new idea, I heard the front door open; Mr Bates came out, and with him was a nurse. After she had

168

seen him mount his horse and depart, she was about to close the door, but I ran up to her.

'How is Helen Burns?'

'Very poorly,' was the answer.

'Is it her Mr Bates has been to see?'

'Yes.'

'And what does he say about her?'

'He says she'll not be here long.'

This phrase, uttered in my hearing yesterday, would have only conveyed the notion that she was about to be removed to Northumberland, to her own home. I should not have suspected that it meant she was dying; but I knew instantly now; it opened clear on my comprehension that Helen Burns was numbering her last days in this world, and that she was going to be taken to the region of spirits, if such region there were. I experienced a shock of horror, then a strong thrill of grief, then a desire – a necessity to see her; and I asked in what room she lay.

'She is in Miss Temple's room,' said the nurse.

'May I go up and speak to her?'

'Oh, no, child! It is not likely; and now it is time for you to come in; you'll catch the fever if you stop out when the dew is falling.'

The nurse closed the front door; I went in by the side entrance which led to the schoolroom: I was just in time; it was nine o'clock, and Miss Miller was calling the pupils to go to bed.

It might be two hours later, probably near eleven, when I – not having been able to fall asleep, and deeming, from the perfect silence of the dormitory, that my companions were all wrapt in profound repose – rose softly, put on my frock over my nightdress, and, without shoes, crept from the apartment, and set off in quest of Miss Temple's room. It was quite at the other end of the house; but I knew my way; and the light of the unclouded summer moon, entering here and there at passage windows, enabled me to find it without difficulty. An odour of camphor and burnt vinegar warned me when I came near the fever room: and I passed its door quickly, fearful lest the nurse who sat up all night should hear me. I dreaded being discovered and sent back; for I *must* see Helen, I must embrace her before she died, I must give her one last kiss, exchange with her one last word.

Having descended a staircase, traversed a portion of the house below, and succeeded in opening and shutting, without noise, two doors, I reached another flight of steps; these I mounted, and then just opposite to me was Miss Temple's room. A light shone through the keyhole, and from under the door; a profound stillness pervaded the vicinity. Coming near, I found the door slightly ajar; probably to admit some fresh air into the close abode of sickness. Indisposed to hesitate, and full of impatient impulses – soul and senses quivering with keen throes – I put it back and looked in. My eye sought Helen, and feared to find death.

Close by Miss Temple's bed, and half covered, with its white curtains, there stood a little crib. I saw the outline of a form under the clothes, but the face was hid by the hangings: the nurse I had spoken to in the garden sat in an easy chair, asleep; an unsnuffed candle burnt dimly on the table. Miss Temple was not to be seen: I knew afterwards that she had been called to a delirious patient in the fever room. I advanced; then paused by the crib side: my hand was on the curtain, but I preferred speaking before I withdrew it. I still recoiled at the dread of seeing a corpse.

'Helen?' I whispered softly; 'are you awake?'

She stirred herself, put back the curtain, and I saw her face, pale, wasted, but quite composed: she looked so little changed that my fear was instantly dissipated.

'Can it be you, Jane?' she asked in her own gentle voice.

'Oh!' I thought, 'she is not going to die; they are mistaken: she could not speak and look so calmly if she were.'

I got on to her crib and kissed her; her forehead was cold, and her cheek both cold and thin, and so were her hand and wrist; but she smiled as of old.

'Why are you come here, Jane? It is past eleven o'clock: I heard it strike some minutes since.'

'I came to see you, Helen: I heard you were very ill, and I could not sleep till I had spoken to you.'

'You came to bid me goodbye, then: you are just in time probably.'

'Are you going somewhere, Helen? Are you going home?'

'Yes; to my long home – my last home.'

'No, no, Helen!' I stopped, distressed.

While I tried to devour my tears, a fit of coughing seized Helen; it did not, however, wake the nurse; when it was over, she lay some minutes exhausted; then she whispered, 'Jane, your little feet are bare; lie down and cover yourself with my quilt.'

I did so: she put her arm over me, and I nestled close to her. After a long silence, she resumed; still whispering, 'I am very happy, Jane; and when you hear that I am dead, you must be sure and not grieve: there is nothing to grieve about. We all must die one day, and the illness which is removing me is not painful; it is gentle and gradual: my mind is at rest. I leave no one to regret me much: I have only a father; and he is lately married, and will not miss me. By dying young, I shall escape great sufferings. I had not qualities or talents to make my way very well in the world: I should have been continually at fault.'

'But where are you going to, Helen? Can you see? Do you know?'

'I believe; I have faith: I am going to God.'

'Where is God? What is God?'

'My Maker and yours, who will never destroy what he created. I rely implicitly on his power, and confide wholly in his goodness: I count the hours till that eventful one arrives which shall restore me to him, reveal him to me.'

'You are sure, then, Helen, that there is such a place as heaven; and that our souls can get to it when we die?'

'I am sure there is a future state; I believe God is good; I can resign my immortal part to him without any misgiving.

171

God is my father; God is my friend: I love him; I believe he loves me.'

'And shall I see you again, Helen, when I die?'

'You will come to the same region of happiness: be received by the same mighty, universal Parent, no doubt, dear Jane.'

Again I questioned; but this time only in thought. 'Where is that region? Does it exist?' And I clasped my arms closer round Helen; she seemed dearer to me than ever; I felt as if I could not let her go; I lay with my face hidden on her neck. Presently she said in the sweetest tone, 'How comfortable I am! That last fit of coughing has tired me a little; I feel as if I could sleep: but don't leave me, Jane; I like to have you near me.'

'I'll stay with you, *dear* Helen: no one shall take me away.'

'Are you warm, darling?'

'Yes.'

'Goodnight, Jane.'

'Goodnight, Helen.'

She kissed me, and I her; and we both soon slumbered.

When I awoke it was day; an unusual movement roused me; I looked up; I was in somebody's arms; the nurse held me; she was carrying me through the passage back to the dormitory. I was not reprimanded for leaving my bed; people had something else to think about: no explanation was afforded then to my many questions; but a day or two afterwards I learned that Miss Temple, on returning to her own room at dawn, had found me laid in a little crib; my face against Helen Burns's shoulder, my arms round her neck. I was asleep, and Helen was – dead.

Her grave is in Brocklebridge churchyard: for fifteen years after her death it was only covered by a grassy mound; but now a gray marble tablet marks the spot, inscribed with her name, and the word '*Resurgam*'.

THE BIBLE

Forsake not an old friend; for the new is not comparable to
him; a new friend is a new wine; when it is old, thou shalt
drink it with pleasure.

BYRON

from *Hours of Idleness*

Friendship is Love without his wings!

ELIZABETH BARRETT BROWNING

'Bows and Curtseys'

My child, we were two children,
Small, merry by childhood's law;
We used to crawl to the hen-house
And hide ourselves in the straw.

We crowed like cocks, and whenever
The passers near us drew –
Cock-a-doodle! they thought
'Twas a real cock that crew.

The boxes about our courtyard
We carpeted to our mind,
And lived there both together –
Kept house in a noble kind.

The neighbour's old cat often
Came to pay us a visit;
We made her a bow and curtsey,
Each with a compliment in it.

After her health we asked,
Our care and regard to evince –
(We have made the very same speeches
To many an old cat since).

ST JOHN IRVINE

When a friend dies, part of yourself dies too.

RICHARD WILBUR

A Game of Catch

Monk and Glennie were playing catch on the side lawn of
the firehouse when Scho caught sight of them. They were
good at it, for seventh-graders, as anyone could see right
away. Monk, wearing a catcher's mitt, would lean easily
sideways and back, with one leg lifted and his throwing
hand almost down to the grass, and then lob the white ball
straight up into the sunlight. Glennie would shield his eyes
with his left hand and, just as the ball fell past him, snag it
with a little dart of his glove. Then he would burn the ball
straight towards Monk, and it would spank into the round
mitt and sit, like a still-life apple on a plate, until Monk
flipped it over into his right hand and, with a negligent flick
of his hanging arm, gave Glennie a fast grounder.

They were going on and on like that, in a kind of slow,
mannered, luxurious dance in the sun, their faces perfectly
blank and entranced, when Glennie noticed Scho dawdling
along the other side of the street and called hello to him.
Scho crossed over and stood at the front edge of the lawn,
near an apple tree, watching.

'Got your glove?' asked Glennie after a time. Scho
obviously hadn't.

'You could give me some easy grounders,' said Scho. 'But
don't burn 'em.'

'All right,' Glennie said. He moved off a little, so the three
of them formed a triangle, and they passed the ball around

for about five minutes, Monk tossing easy grounders to Scho, Scho throwing to Glennie, and Glennie burning them in to Monk. After a while, Monk began to throw them back to Glennie once or twice before he let Scho have his grounder, and finally Monk gave Scho a fast, bumpy grounder that hopped over his shoulder and went into the brake on the other side of the street.

'Not so hard,' called Scho as he ran across to get it.

'You should've had it,' Monk shouted.

It took Scho a little while to find the ball among the ferns and dead leaves, and when he saw it, he grabbed it up and threw it towards Glennie. It struck the trunk of the apple tree, bounced back at an angle, and rolled steadily and stupidly on to the cement apron in front of the firehouse, where one of the trucks was parked. Scho ran hard and stopped it just before it rolled under the truck, and this time he carried it back to his former position on the lawn and threw it carefully to Glennie.

'I got an idea,' said Glennie. 'Why don't Monk and I catch for five minutes more, and then you can borrow one of our gloves?'

'That's all right with me,' said Monk. He socked his fist into his mitt, and Glennie burned one in.

'All right,' Scho said, and went over and sat under the tree. There in the shade he watched them resume their skilful play. They threw lazily fast or lazily slow – high, low, or wide – and always handsomely, their expression serene, changeless and forgetful. When Monk missed a low backhand catch, he walked indolently after the ball and, hardly even looking, flung it side-arm for an imaginary put-out. After a good while of this, Scho said, 'Isn't it five minutes yet?'

'One minute to go,' said Monk, with a fraction of a grin.

Scho stood up and watched the ball slap back and forth for several minutes more, and then he turned and pulled himself up into the crotch of the tree.

'Where you going?' Monk asked.

'Just up the tree,' Scho said.

'I guess he doesn't want to catch,' said Monk.

Scho went up and up through the fat light-grey branches until they grew slender and bright and gave under him. He found a place where several supple branches were knit to make a dangerous chair, and sat there with his head coming out of the leaves into the sunlight. He could see the two other boys down below, the ball going back and forth between them as if they were bowling on the grass, and Glennie's crew-cut head looking like a sea urchin.

'I found a wonderful seat up here,' Scho said loudly. 'If I don't fall out.' Monk and Glennie didn't look up or comment, and so he began jouncing gently in his chair of branches and singing 'Yo-ho, heave ho' in an exaggerated way.

'Do you know what, Monk?' he announced in a few moments. 'I can make you two guys do anything I want. Catch that ball, Monk! Now you catch it, Glennie!'

'I was going to catch it anyway,' Monk suddenly said. 'You're not making anybody do anything when they're already going to do it anyway.'

'I made you say what you just said,' Scho replied joyfully.

'No, you didn't,' said Monk, still throwing and catching but now less serenely absorbed in the game.

'That's what I wanted you to say,' Scho said.

The ball bounded off the rim of Monk's mitt and ploughed into a gladiolus bed beside the firehouse, and Monk ran to get it while Scho jounced in his treetop and sang, 'I wanted you to miss that. Anything you do is what I wanted you to do.'

'Let's quit for a minute,' Glennie suggested.

'We might as well, until the peanut gallery shuts up,' Monk said.

They went over and sat cross-legged in the shade of the tree. Scho looked down between his legs and saw them on the dim, spotty ground, saying nothing to one another. Glennie soon began abstractedly spinning his glove beween his palms; Monk pulled his nose and stared out across the lawn.

'I want you to mess around with your nose, Monk,' said Scho, giggling. Monk withdrew his hand from his face.

'Do that with your glove, Glennie,' Scho persisted. 'Monk, I want you to pull up hunks of grass and chew on it.'

Glennie looked up and saw a self-delighted, intense face staring down at him through the leaves. 'Stop being a dope and come down and we'll catch for a few minutes,' he said.

Scho hesitated, and then said, in a tentatively mocking voice, 'That's what I wanted you to say.'

'All right, then, nuts to you,' said Glennie.

'Why don't you keep quiet and stop bothering people?' Monk asked.

'I made you say that,' Scho replied softly.

'Shut up,' Monk said.

'I made you say that, and I want you to be standing there looking sore. And I want you to climb up the tree. I'm making you do it.'

Monk was scrambling up through the branches, awkward in his haste, and getting snagged on twigs. His face was furious and foolish, and he kept telling Scho to shut up, shut up, shut up, while the other's exuberant and panicky voice poured down upon his head.

'*Now* you shut up or you'll be sorry,' Monk said, breathing hard as he reached up and threatened to shake the cradle of slight branches in which Scho was sitting.

'I *want* –' Scho screamed as he fell. Two lower branches broke his rustling, crackling fall, but he landed on his back with a deep thud and lay still, with a strangled look on his face and his eyes clenched. Glennie knelt down and asked breathlessly, 'Are you OK Scho? Are you OK?' while Monk swung down through the leaves crying that honestly he hadn't even touched him, the crazy guy just let go. Scho doubled up and turned over on his right side, and now both the other boys knelt beside him, pawing at his shoulder and begging to know how he was.

Then Scho rolled away from them and sat partly up, still struggling to get his wind but forcing a species of smile on to his face.

'I'm sorry, Scho,' Monk said. 'I didn't meant to make you fall.'

Scho's voice came out weak and gravelly, in gasps. 'I meant – you to do it. You – had to. You can't do – anything – unless I want – you to.'

Glennie and Monk looked helplessly at him as he sat there, breathing a bit more easily and smiled fixedly, with tears in his eyes. Then they picked up their gloves and the ball, walked over to the street, and went slowly away down the pavement, Monk punching his fist into the mitt, Glennie juggling the ball between glove and hand.

From under the apple tree, Scho, still bent over a little for lack of breath, croaked after them in triumph and misery, 'I want you to do whatever you're going to do for the whole rest of your life!'

ACKNOWLEDGEMENTS

The editor and publishers wish to thank the following for permission to use copyright material;

BookBlast Ltd on behalf of the author for Aamer Hussein, 'Dreaming of Java' in *Mirror to the Sun*, Mantra Publishing Ltd. © Aamer Hussein 1994, 1997;

David Higham Associates on behalf of the authors for extracts from Elizabeth McCraken, *The Giant's House*, Jonathan Cape (1996); and Muriel Spark, 'The Twins' from *The Stories of Muriel Spark*, Penguin Books (1985);

Harcourt Brace & Company for Richard Wilbur, 'A Game of Catch' from *A Game of Catch*, originally in *The New Yorker*, 1953 © 1994 by Richard Wilbur;

A. M. Heath on behalf of the Estate of the author for a quote by George Orwell, *Animal Farm*. © Mark Hamilton as the Literary Executor of the late Sonia Brownell Orwell and Martin Secker and Warburg Ltd;

MBA Literary Agents on behalf of the author for an extract from Elspeth Sandys, *Finding Out*, Vintage NZ (1991);

Oxford University Press for Fleur Adcock, 'A Hymn to Friendship' from *Time-Zones*. © Fleur Adcock 1991;

Punch Ltd for Major E. De Stein, 'Elegy On the Death of Bingo Our Trench Dog', *Punch*, Sept. 18 1918;

Random House UK for W. H. Davies, 'A Child's Pet' from *The Complete Poems of W. H. Davies*, Jonathan Cape; and Angus Wilson, 'Christmas Day in the Workhouse' from *Such Darling Dodos and Other Stories*, Secker and Warburg (1950);

Nann du Sautoy for Nann Morgenstern, 'The Befriender'. © Nann Morgenstern 1997;

Sheil Land Associates Ltd on behalf of the Estate of the author for extracts from Brigid Brophy, *King of a Rainy Country*. © Brigid Brophy 1956;

The Society of Authors on behalf of Literary Trustees of the author for Walter de la Mare, 'Miss Duveen' from *Best Stories of Walter de la Mare*, Faber and Faber (1983);

Every effort has been made to trace the copyright holders but if any have been inadvertently overlooked the publishers will be pleased to make the necessary arrangement at the first opportunity.

CHILDHOOD · FRIENDSHIP · FIRS